SCIENTIFIC AMERICAN EXPLORES BIG IDEAS

The Science of Identity

I0794112

Published in 2023 by Scientific American Educational Publishing
in association with **The Rosen Publishing Group**
2544 Clinton Street, Buffalo NY 14224

Contains material from Scientific American®, a division of Springer Nature America, Inc., reprinted by permission, as well as original material from The Rosen Publishing Group®.

Copyright © 2023 Scientific American® and Rosen Publishing Group®.

All rights reserved.

First Edition

Scientific American
Lisa Pallatroni: Project Editor

Rosen Publishing
Erica Grove: Compiling Editor
Michael Moy: Senior Graphic Designer

Cataloging-in-Publication Data
Names: Scientific American.
Title: The Science of identity / Scientific American.
Description: New York : Scientific American Educational, 2023. | Series: Scientific american explores big ideas| Includes bibliographic information, glossary and index.
Identifiers: ISBN 9781725348943 (pbk) | ISBN 9781725348950 (library bound) | ISBN 9781725348967 (ebook)
Subjects: LCSH: Identity – Juvenile literature | Personality– Juvenile literature | Prejudices– Juvenile literature | Racism– Juvenile literature | Social perception– Juvenile literature | Stereotypes– Juvenile literature
Classification: LCC BF323.S63 S35 2023 | DDC 303.3/85 –dc23

Manufactured in the United States of America
Websites listed were live at the time of publication.

Cover: sdecoret/Shutterstock.com

CPSIA Compliance Information: Batch # SACW23.
For Further Information contact Rosen Publishing at 1-800-237-9932.

CONTENTS

INTRODUCTION

Your identity is made up of a wide range of personality traits, beliefs, and qualities–both physical and internal–that make you who you are. It affects how others see you and how you see yourself. But what determines which traits, qualities, and beliefs you will possess or be drawn to in other people? Researchers in medicine, biology, and the social sciences have long attempted to find ways of answering this question. This has involved examining genetic makeup, brain activity, emotional responses, and social structures in order to find patterns that can help explain how identity is formed. While this research can play a role in helping people to understand themselves and those around them, it may also help to address some of the more problematic aspects of identity, such as stereotyping others based on the characteristics that make up their identity.

The articles in this book look at a wide range of studies and opinions from researchers, doctors, and academics to shed light on what variables affect one's identity. Section 1, "The Science of Stereotyping," examines what causes people to form stereotypical views of others and how to combat these oversimplified and often derogatory attitudes. Section 2, "Understanding Gender and Sexuality through Science," looks at research on what we know and don't know about the factors that determine sexuality and gender and their associated characteristics. Section 3, "Using Science to Explain Your Tastes and Beliefs," considers the research behind our cultural preferences–including music and food–and our systems of belief, such as politics. Section 4, "The Factors that Shape Your Personality," contemplates what causes us to develop a particular personality and how well your personality can be understood through testing and assessment. Through breaking the subject of identity down into its different aspects and considering a variety of perspectives on how these characteristics are formed, the articles in this book attempt to shed light on this multifaceted and complicated subject.

Section 1: The Science of Stereotyping

What Drives Subconscious Racial Prejudice?

By Jeneen Interlandi

Last fall, Emile Bruneau, a cognitive neuroscientist from M.I.T., was in Budapest running a series of behavioral experiments designed to measure anti-Roma bias in a cohort of Hungarian schoolteachers. Anti-Roma bias is rampant in schools throughout Central and Eastern Europe; in many countries, including Hungary, it takes the form of full-blown segregation. Bruneau wanted to see if he could not only quantify this bias, but also break it down into its constituent parts, and from there, figure out how to alleviate it.

Here's how the experiment would work:

Each teacher would be made to sit in front a computer screen and communicate with a student whom they believed was in another room, completing a numbers and logic quiz as part of a study of online learning habits. The teachers would have the option of giving positive, neutral or negative feedback at various intervals throughout the quiz. The "students" were really actors–some of them Roma and some of them non-Roma–that Emile's team had pre-recorded assuming different postures (attentive, bored, frustrated, pleased and so on). The hypothesis was that the teachers who tested as more overtly biased on psychological assessments, which Bruneau had administered on a previous visit, would be more inclined to give negative feedback and less inclined to praise or encourage the Roma students.

Bruneau wanted to keep the true intentions of the study hidden from the teachers so as not to trigger any feigned responses. "We want them to believe that these are real students that they're interacting with, students who are sitting at a similar computer screen in a nearby building," he told his research assistants. "So just think of things you would do if that were true. You'd maybe text the person in that other room, or wait to hear from them before hitting the start button."

Because here's the thing about racial prejudice: while most people would agree that it's a root cause of racial inequality, few would cop to being guilty of it themselves. We live on a planet rife with ethnic tension; racial prejudice is both the loud and conspicuous engine driving that tension, and the elusive ghost inside the machine. It is everywhere and nowhere at once. And it's not just the gap between what we think and what we say that trips us up. It's the gap between what we think and what we *think* we think. Discrepancies between our conscious and subconscious impede our capacity for impartial judgment and our ability to recognize that impediment, even when it's smacking us in the face.

Behavioral experiments like the one Bruneau was conducting are just one way to circumvent this paradox. As crude as they sometimes sound, they can be eerily prescient. For example, in one 2005 study, 50 police officers were presented with a photograph of a man holding either a gun or a cell phone, and forced to decide very quickly whether to shoot (in case of a gun) or withhold fire (in case of a cell phone). The officers were more likely to mistakenly shoot unarmed black suspects than unarmed white suspects (although the bias went away after extensive training).

Neuroimaging studies have also demonstrated clear differences in how our brains respond to people whose ethnicity differs from our own. For example, activity in the amygdala, a region associated with fear and threat detection, is routinely found to be higher in white subjects when they view black faces than it is when they view white ones. Likewise, in a 2009 study, when white participants watched a white hand being pierced by a needle, motor activity in the observer's hand was suppressed as if they had been pricked themselves. This didn't happen when watching black hands get pricked.

A third tool researchers can use to probe the subconscious is the IAT, or implicit association test (sometimes referred to as the "racist test"). It measures exactly what its name suggests: subconscious associations that people make between various images and concepts. It does this by comparing how long a person takes to match certain words and images to one another. A person might readily link the word "safe" with a white face, for example, but take longer to link it to a black face. That difference in time is seen as a reliable measure of unconscious bias because it takes more time to link words and images that the mind deems incompatible.

There are several permutations of the IAT, each one measuring a different strain of racial bias: the extent to which we subscribe to stereotypes, for example, or the extent to which we attribute (or fail to attribute) human-specific emotions to different racial groups. Bruneau administered several different tests like these to his teachers in Budapest before beginning the anti-Roma bias experiment. After the experiment, he would compare the results of both exams to see which aspects of racial bias–stereotyping, dehumanization, or affect (the amount of warmth we feel towards members of a given racial group)–were most predictive of the teachers' treatment of Roma students, and of their support for school segregation in general.

"What we hope to have at the end is a validated anti-Roma bias battery," he said. "And then we can use that to decide which aspects of bias we should target in the intervention phase."

I observed Bruneau's experiment first hand. It was quiet. A few research assistants milled about while a teacher–a young woman with short brown hair, in jeans and a soft blue shirt–sat in front of a computer console completing what she believed was a study of online learning habits. I wondered if she suspected the true aim of the study, and how she would react if it were suddenly revealed to her. She did not look racist. I guess nobody does. I guess that's the point.

Afterwards, I grabbed coffee with Hannah Szekeres, Bruneau's research assistant. Szekeres was a Hungarian Jew; she had grown up in Budapest and was now living in Tel Aviv and pursuing a Ph.D. in social psychology. She had returned to her native city to run the teacher study for Bruneau, and between that and the latest round of violence in Gaza, she had been thinking almost nonstop about inter-group conflict and racial prejudice.

We got to comparing the U.S. to Israel to Hungary. Ferguson, Missouri was tipping into chaos just then. It would be a few months before the grand jury issued its decision not to indict Darren Wilson, the white police officer responsible for the shooting death of Michael Brown, an unarmed black teenager, but riots had already broken out. As I told Szekeres, my Facebook feed had been flooded with reactions of every caliber: lots of outrage and solidarity with the black community, but also plenty of white people insisting that the shooting had nothing to do with race. *He robbed a convenience store then ran from police*, the argument went. *He brought it on himself.* I told her I was shocked that anyone could fail to see the role racial bias was playing in their own thinking.

"That's nothing," she said. "Here, even the liberals will compare the Roma to animals." The way Szekeres sees it, there are three types of people: those who are openly prejudiced, those who insist that they hold all groups as equal, and those who understood that we all harbor biases–some conscious, some subconscious–and that what matters is how we deal with them. She hoped that the study would help pull more people into this third group, and that over time, that shift in thinking would lead to real change. "It's really great and important for the Roma to have equal access to education," she said. "But that doesn't solve the whole problem because once they are educated, they still have to deal with the majority's perception of them."

It was too soon to guess at the results of the teacher experiment, but Szerkeres had had some interesting exchanges with the subjects. "We asked this one very nice girl if she thought the education profile was Roma," she told me. "She said, 'Oh, you mean because the score was so low? Yeah, I thought so.' And then we asked her at the end if she thought she would have rated the student differently if the students were Roma vs. non-Roma, and she said no immediately."

They all said no to that question, Szekeres told me. Without even thinking about it.

Reporting for this post was supported by the Pulitzer Center on Crisis Reporting.

The views expressed are those of the author(s) and are not necessarily those of Scientific American.

About the Author

Jeneen Interlandi is a New York City–based journalist who writes about health, science and the environment.

How to Unlearn Racism

By Abigail Libers

In February 2016 I sat in a conference room on the Upper East Side of Manhattan with about 35 other people attempting to answer what seemed like a straightforward question: *What is racism?*

I—a white, able-bodied, cis-gendered woman in my 30s—thought that racism was prejudice against an individual because of race or ethnicity. That's why I had signed up for the Undoing Racism Workshop, a two-and-a-half-day antiracist training that analyzes race and power structures in the U.S.: I wanted to gain a better understanding of why some people have so much contempt toward those who are different from them. My yearning for answers came from personal experience with discrimination as a Jewish woman and the daughter of immigrants; my parents fled to the U.S. from the former Soviet Union in 1979. Growing up in a small town in upstate New York followed by an even smaller, more rural town in Georgia, I was picked on and often felt "othered."

The workshop was hosted by the People's Institute for Survival and Beyond (PISAB), an organization that was founded 40 years ago by community organizers who wanted to create a more equitable society by addressing the root causes of racism. Our leaders—a Black man, a white woman and a Latina woman—called on each of us to share our definitions of racism. People's responses were all over the map, from "a mean-spirited, close-minded way of thinking" to "discrimination based on someone's skin color or ethnic background." The trainers validated each of our responses before pointing out how varied they were and explaining that few of us had identified racism as a web of institutional power and oppression based on skin color. Not having a simple or agreed-on definition of racism makes it easier to keep racism in place. To undo racism, they said, we need a common language that ties together individual and systemic factors. Hearing racism described as a power hierarchy was eye-opening for me. Having been marginalized myself, I thought

I was sensitive toward other groups who faced discrimination. I thought I got it.

Over the past year, America has been reckoning with racism on a scale that has not been seen since the civil-rights movement. The killings of George Floyd, Ahmaud Arbery, Breonna Taylor and others sparked protests against systemic racism and police violence that have drawn multiracial participation. Some white Americans attended Black Lives Matter protests for the first time—the movement has been active since 2013—and saw up close the police brutality they previously only read about or witnessed through short video clips on phone screens. These experiences were a tiny window into the reality of violence and oppression that Black people endure. The pandemic further emphasizes the racial disparities that people are protesting, with Black, Latinx and Indigenous communities disproportionately affected by COVID-19. It has become widely discussed that police violence and virus deaths are not disparate issues—they are both embedded in a pervasive system of racism.

PISAB's definition of racism (which is similar to that of other antiracism organizations such as the Racial Equity Institute) is race prejudice plus power. It describes how individual and systemic racism are tied together. All of us have individual race prejudice: anyone can prejudge a person based on race alone. But what makes racism different from individual prejudice is who has institutional power. White people control our government systems and institutions in every sector, from law enforcement and education to health care and the media, leading to laws and policies that can advantage white people while disadvantaging everyone else.

White people's dominance in our systems is why you may have heard people refer to the U.S. as a white supremacist society. In this context, white supremacy does not refer to hate groups such as neo-Nazis and the Ku Klux Klan but rather an entire *system* where one group has all the advantages. "Racism *is* white supremacy," says Joseph Barndt, an organizer and core trainer with PISAB and author of *Understanding and Dismantling Racism: The Twenty-First*

Century Challenge to White America. "It's empowering one alleged racial group over another and creating systems to reinforce that."

As more white people seek to confront and undo racism in their own lives, they are figuring out how to "do the work." In recent years implicit bias trainings, which aim to expose people to the negative associations and stereotypes they hold and express unconsciously, have been widely used to raise people's awareness of racism in workplaces. But addressing bias is not sufficient for confronting the racist systems, ideas and legacies that are present in our day-to-day lives. There is no one-size-fits-all solution, but research shows that undoing racism often starts with understanding what race and racism actually are. It is also crucial to develop a positive racial identity; to feel—not just intellectualize—how racism harms *all* of us and, finally, to learn how to break prejudice habits and become an active antiracist. Doing so, however, is not accomplished in a weekend. For me, one of the first steps was unlearning false ideas about the basis of racial categories.

Seeing Whiteness in the Origins of Race

Race is deeply embedded in our society, yet it is persistently misunderstood to be a biological construct rather than a cultural one. The concept of racial categories is actually quite modern, explains Crystal Fleming, a professor of sociology at Stony Brook University and author of *How to Be Less Stupid about Race*: "If we think about our species existing for at least a few hundred thousand years, it's only in the last several centuries that we see the historical emergence of the idea of race." This is a history that most Americans are not taught in school. False classifications of humans that would later be called "races" began in the 16th and 17th centuries with Christian clergy questioning whether "Blacks" and "Indians" were human. As colonial expansion and slavery increased, religion was used to justify classifying Black people and other people of color as "pagan and soulless." But as many of them were converted to Christianity and the Age of Enlightenment took off in the 1700s, religion lost its legitimizing power.

Instead "science" was used to justify the enslavement of Africans and the genocide of Indigenous peoples, which had already been occurring in British colonies for more than a century. Johann Friedrich Blumenbach, a German anthropologist and comparative anatomist, is known for proposing one of the earliest classifications of the human race, which he wrote about in the late 1700s.

His measurement of skulls from around the world led him to divide humans into five groups, which were later simplified by anthropologists into three categories: Caucasoids, Mongoloids and Negroids. It did not seem to matter that some prominent scientists, including Charles Darwin, dismissed a biological basis for race over the next century. Many scientists dedicated themselves to proving a false racial hierarchy in which "Caucasians" were superior to other races.

In the U.S., political and intellectual leaders reinforced the false ideology that Africans were biologically inferior to other races and therefore best suited for slavery. After Bacon's Rebellion in 1676, which had united white and Black indentured servants, Virginia lawmakers began to make legal distinctions between "white" and "Black" people. Poor white indentured servants who served their term could go free and own land; Black servants were committed to lifelong servitude. With the Naturalization Act of 1790, Congress codified white racial advantage into law by limiting citizenship by naturalization to "free white persons," namely white men. Women, people of color and indentured servants were excluded.

With white superiority cemented firmly into law, the social and political power of *whiteness* was born. As a category, it was increasingly associated with resources and power: explicit laws and practices that created whiteness as a requirement for being able to live in certain neighborhoods, to be able to vote, to own land, to testify in court before a jury. The legacy of "scientific" racism persists to this day.

Although biology has shown that there are no genetically distinct races, racial *identity*—how you and others perceive your race—is very real, as are its ramifications. In a white-dominant society like America, white people tend to be unaware of their identity and may think of themselves as neutral, as nonracial. According to the work of psychologist Janet Helms, who published six stages of white racial identity development in 1999, the first stage is defined by a lack of awareness of cultural and institutional racism. This stage is also characterized by being "color-blind"—imagining one does not see people's differences and viewing that as a positive trait others should aspire to.

As scholar and activist Peggy McIntosh notes in a 1989 article, this lack of awareness is common. She describes white privilege as an "invisible package of unearned assets that I can count on cashing in each day, but about which I was 'meant' to remain oblivious. White privilege is like an invisible weightless knapsack of special provisions, maps, passports, codebooks, visas, clothes, tools, and blank checks."

To unlearn racism then, white people must first examine their racial identity. Black scholars and writers of color have known this for more than a century; their survival depended on it. Frederick Douglass, W.E.B. Du Bois, James Baldwin, Audre Lorde, Angela Davis, Ta-Nehisi Coates and many others have observed, analyzed and written about whiteness for generations. Du Bois made observations about whiteness in 1899 with his sociological study *The Philadelphia Negro* and in 1935 with his book, *Black Reconstruction in America.* Recently Ijeoma Oluo, author of *So You Want to Talk about Race*, wrote in a popular Medium article: "I know white culture better than most white people know white culture."

It has only been in the past few decades that white scholars have turned the lens on themselves with the emergence of Critical Whiteness Studies (CWS), a growing academic field that aims to examine the structures of white supremacy and privilege and to investigate the meaning of white privilege and how it is connected to complicity in racism. According to Barbara Applebaum, a professor of philosophy and education at Syracuse University, CWS shifts the focus, and thus the blame, from the victims of racism to the perpetrators. As she explains, "it names the elephant in the room—the construction and maintenance of whiteness."

Workshops Aren't Enough

Over the past 20 years or so initiatives to address racism have focused heavily on implicit bias trainings. A growing body of cognitive research demonstrates how these hidden biases impact our attitudes and actions, which result in real-world consequences such as racial profiling.

The trainings, which are often sponsored by human resources departments but delivered to employees by outside consulting firms, may consist of modules that walk people through what implicit bias is and where it comes from, how it shows up in the workplace, how it is measured (typically through the Implicit Association Test) and how to reduce it. Over the past decade these trainings have been widely used in the law-enforcement industry as well as in the tech industry, with companies such as Facebook and Google putting thousands of employees through trainings. More recently, antibias trainings have been implemented in schools for teachers.

While these sessions may be useful in exposing people's hidden biases, those revelations have not been shown to result in long-term behavioral change on an individual or systemic level. In a 2018 paper published in *Anthropology Now*, Harvard University sociologist Frank Dobbin writes: "Hundreds of studies dating back to the 1930s suggest that antibias training does not reduce bias, alter behavior or change the workplace."

A recent meta-analysis of 492 studies (with a total of 87,418 participants) on the effectiveness of implicit bias training found weak effects on unconscious bias. The authors note that "most studies focused on producing short-term changes with brief, single-session manipulations" and that most trainings "produced trivial changes in behavior." The authors conclude that changes in implicit bias are possible, but they do not necessarily translate into changes in explicit bias or behavior, and there is a significant lack of research on the long-term effects.

"Implicit bias trainings raise awareness, but they also tell people, 'This is just how the brain works,'" says Rachel Godsil, co-founder and co-director of the Perception Institute, an organization that works with social scientists to identify the efficacy of interventions to address implicit bias, racial anxiety and the effects of stereotypes. "It kind of leaves people feeling like they are let off the hook." It's not that your brain is hard-wired to be racist, but it is programmed to put people into categories. And the categories that have been constructed in the U.S., Godsil explains, have meanings that tend to be negative for people from marginalized groups. She emphasizes that part of what it means to unlearn racism is to delink stereotypes from identities and absolute truths: "You're not trying to be color-blind or pretend that these categories don't exist, but you don't presume you know anything about a person based on their identity."

Antiracism trainings, such as the Undoing Racism Workshop, differ significantly from implicit bias trainings in that they are more intense on both an intellectual and emotional level. Because they are not done in a corporate setting, the discussions tend to be more honest and raw. In the PISAB training I attended, we took a hard look at white supremacy and our role in upholding it. After reviewing a history of racism in the U.S., the trainers discussed individual and institutional racial attitudes, oppression and privilege, and how institutions implicitly or explicitly perpetuate racism. We were empowered to be "gatekeepers"—leaders who can affect change in our workplaces and communities.

PISAB's methodology is rooted in community organizing principles that the group's founders honed for decades. Their approach is based on philosopher Paulo Freire's pedagogy, which focuses on linking knowledge to action so people can make real change in their communities. Other antiracist trainings, such as the one offered by Crossroads Antiracism Organizing & Training, provide a similar approach. In contrast, Robin DiAngelo, author of *White*

Fragility: Why It's So Hard for White People to Talk about Racism, who has received much attention in recent months, gives "keynote presentations" that are more focused on individual prejudice and white privilege.

Whereas these trainings can be powerful in many ways, it is unclear to what degree they are effective—and if they are, how and why they work. A 2015 study published in *Race and Social Problems* aimed to measure the impact of PISAB's training and found that approximately 60 percent of participants engaged in racial equity work after completing the Undoing Racism Workshop. "These trainings are well intentioned, but we don't know if they work, because there aren't randomized controlled experiments to prove that they do," says Patricia Devine, a professor of psychology who studies prejudice at the University of Wisconsin–Madison.

Trainings on implicit bias, diversity and antiracism may be limited in their efficacy in part because they tend to be brief one-off events. Promising research by Devine in 2013 showed that prejudices and biases can be more successfully unlearned through longer-term intervention. The 12-week longitudinal study was based on the premise that implicit bias is like a habit that can be broken through the following steps: becoming aware of implicit bias, developing concern about the effects of that bias and using strategies to reduce bias—specifically, ones that replace biased reactions with responses that reflect one's nonprejudiced goals.

The researchers argue that the motivation to "break the prejudice habit" comes from two sources: First, you have to be aware of your biases, and second, you have to be *concerned* about the consequences of your biases to be motivated to make the effort needed to eliminate them. Recent research has shown that interacting with a wide variety of racial groups can help people care more about racial justice. For instance, a 2018 review suggested that increased contact among racial groups deepens psychological investment in equality by making people more empathetic.

For Fleming, who has educated thousands of university students, teaching implicit bias within the context of a comprehensive, three-month course "is far more effective than being dragged into a diversity training for an afternoon," she says. "People have to feel inspired. They have to feel a desire to critically reflect on not just their biases but on their socialization and conditioning and to be part of a positive social transformation. You can't force that on anyone."

Feeling the Harms of Racism

The inspiration that Fleming speaks to is what motivates me to unlearn racism, to reeducate myself on swaths of American history, and to open my eyes to whiteness and white supremacy. But the process of unlearning is only the first step, and it needs to translate into a commitment to practices such as breaking white silence and bringing an antiracist lens to my work. That is only possible, and sustainable, by building empathy and *feeling* the ways in which racism is not just harmful for people of color–it hurts white people, too.

This realization didn't hit me until I took PISAB's workshop for a second time in 2019. I had signed up at the urging of Stoop Nilsson, a social worker and racial reeducation coach who shows white people how to become antiracist leaders in their communities. During the workshop, Barndt, one of the trainers, pointed out how easy it can be for white people to think racism does not harm them. But "the truth is, with racism we lose, too," he said. "All of humanity loses. With the end of racism, we get our lives back."

H. Shellac Versey, a critical health researcher and professor of psychology at Fordham University, studies how white supremacy culture impacts the mental health of both white and nonwhite populations. In a 2019 paper, she and her co-authors explain how white people are harmed by the myth of meritocracy–the idea that working hard and pulling yourself up by your bootstraps leads to success. When this does not happen (for example, if you do not land a promotion you worked hard for), it threatens your worldview and leads to significant stress, research shows.

Versey notes that many white people oppose social health programs such as the Affordable Care Act that would actually benefit them, in part because they believe these programs are designed to benefit people of color. In his recent book *Dying of Whiteness*, physician Jonathan Metzl writes about how some white Americans support politicians who promote policies that increase their risk of sickness and death.

Another way we are all harmed on a day-to-day basis is through white supremacy culture. As Kenneth Jones and Tema Okun write in the book *Dismantling Racism: A Workbook for Social Change Groups*, the characteristics of white supremacy culture include perfectionism, a sense of urgency, defensiveness, quantity over quality, paternalism, either/or thinking, power hoarding, individualism, and more.

Understanding and *feeling* how racism hurts me—even though it is a mere fraction of the pain people of color experience—is part of what helps me internalize the motivation I need to consistently work to undo it. I wonder if white supremacy culture contributes to my elevated anxiety levels, which manifest as migraine headaches and torn-up cuticles. I am more clearly connecting white supremacy culture with climate change denial as well as the paternalism and overly rigid thinking I have experienced in various jobs.

Working with Nilsson is helping me create a positive racial identity of my own—as both a white person and a Russian Jew. Our country prides itself on being a melting pot, but much gets lost in the assimilation to whiteness and white supremacy culture. Markers of ethnic identity such as language, food, culture and music are discouraged; those from a non–Western European heritage are often vilified. In my family, my parents were so committed to learning English that they hardly ever spoke Russian around the house. I never learned it. It saddens me that I can't speak to my own parents in their native language and that I still know so little about our heritage. Recently my mom became frustrated trying to remember a word in English to describe how she was feeling; I worry that her last words will be in Russian, and I'll have no idea what they mean.

In the midst of COVID-19, a high-stakes election season and racial protest movements that illuminate issues affecting everyone, many Americans are reevaluating what matters most. White people may be waking up to areas of their lives that were previously inaccessible to them and to histories and literature and legacies that have long been excluded from school curriculums. This awakening may lead people to work on creating a positive racial identity away from white supremacism, one based on fully acknowledging the power of whiteness in our society and using that knowledge to pursue equality and justice for everyone. Skipping that step risks giving up or doing even more harm; shame and self-loathing are not effective motivators and can inhibit the strength and stamina needed to push for systemic change.

Having been in this process myself for several years, I am certain of only one thing: that antiracism is a lifelong practice. In her book *Why Are All the Black Kids Sitting Together in the Cafeteria?*, psychologist Beverly Daniel Tatum compares racism to smog, writing that it is something we all breathe in; no one is immune to it. Attempting to unlearn racism has meant becoming aware of each inhalation–and doing my best to exhale less of it.

About the Author

Abigail Libers is a freelance journalist and editor based in New York.

Stereotypes Harm Black Lives and Livelihoods, but Research Suggests Ways to Improve Things

By Katy Milkman, Kassie Brabaw

The Black Lives Matter protests shaking the world have thankfully brought renewed attention not just to police brutality but to the broader role of racism in our society. Research suggests some roots of racism lie in the stereotypes we hold about different groups. And those stereotypes can affect everything from the way police diagnose danger to who gets interviewed for jobs to which students get attention from professors. Negative stereotypes harm Black Americans at every turn. To reduce their pernicious effects, it's important to first understand how stereotypes work and just how pervasive they are.

Modupe Akinola, an associate professor at Columbia Business School, studies racial bias, workforce diversity and stress. Recently, Katy Milkman, a professor at the Wharton School at the University of Pennsylvania, got to chat with Akinola about how stereotypes are formed, how they affect consequential decisions and how we can combat negative stereotypes.

[*An edited transcript of the interview follows.*]

Q: Let's start at the beginning. What is a stereotype?

A: A stereotype is a snap judgment we make about a person or about a thing that can influence our decision-making. Every day we get millions and millions of bits of information in our head that associate good and bad with certain people or groups or things. And anytime we then see those people, groups or things, that association comes immediately to our mind.

Q: Why do you think we do this?

A: We're processing so much information all the time; we need these mental shortcuts to allow us to navigate the world. If not, we wouldn't be able to function, quite frankly. We have to make quick judgments to make life easier and to simplify. But any type of shortcut can have its pros and cons.

Q: Could you talk about some of the research connecting stereotyping with racism?

A: One of my favorite sets of studies examines stereotyping as it relates to policing. I grew up in New York City. And we heard a lot about Amadou Diallo, who was an unarmed Black man who was shot by police, because they thought he was carrying a gun–when in actuality, he raised his hand, and he had a wallet.

Joshua Correll, [now at the University of Colorado Boulder], and his colleagues wanted to look at whether the stereotypes associating Black people with danger could play a role in how a mistake like that could be made. The news we see regularly shows crime rates being higher for certain populations, mostly minority populations,. And so this creates an automatic stereotype that a Black man would be more linked to danger than a white man, because you don't see those same associations for white people.

Correll came up with a computerized shooter bias exercise that showed pictures of targets, Black and white men, carrying objects, either weapons or regular objects like a Coke can or a wallet. When you saw a person and the object, you had to click on whether or not to shoot. He found that civilians were more likely to shoot unarmed Black men, relative to unarmed white men and even *armed* white men, which was attributed to the stereotypes associating Black people with danger.

I found that study fascinating, because it showed just how powerful these associations can be. I did some follow-up research, because I wanted to see if stress affects that decision-making process. I stressed out police officers and had them engage in the shooting exercise.

The interesting thing is: I saw that under stress, officers were more accurate. They were able to discern whether to shoot an armed Black man and did that better in terms of not shooting unarmed Black men. However, they were less likely to shoot armed white men, which I think demonstrates the power of stereotypes, because there isn't a stereotype of white and danger.

Stereotypes work in two ways: they can harm some groups, and they can protect others.

Q: Are there any other studies about stereotyping that you think people might find illuminating?

A: My favorite are audit studies, where you observe real-world behavior. There have been audit studies where people go to car dealerships to see if people are treated differently and about who gets mortgages and things like that.

One audit study was testing ads in the newspaper, which were advertising entry-level positions. [The researchers] sent candidate résumés to these job ads, which were identical, and changed the names on the résumés to signal race. "Lakisha" and "Jamal" were Black-sounding names that were tested and pretested to ensure they would signal race versus a name like "Catherine," which would be a more white-sounding name. They waited to see who called back for which candidates. The Lakishas and Jamals received fewer callbacks for an interview than the white-sounding names.

Again, this behavior is attributed to stereotypes. We make presumptions and snap judgments about who might be more qualified for a job, who might do well in a job, even in the context of identical information.

Q: Would you be willing to describe a little bit of the work we've done together on the role of stereotyping in academia?

A: Certainly. We–you, I and Dolly Chugh [of the Stern School of Business at New York University]–wanted to see if racial or gender stereotypes impact the pathway to academia. As you're applying or thinking about getting a Ph.D., often you'll reach out to a professor and ask, "Are you taking graduate students?" or "Can I learn more about your research?" We get these e-mails, all the time, asking for time on our schedule. And we wanted to see if professors would differentially respond to these requests, depending on the race and gender of the requester.

We sent e-mails to around 6,500 professors across the country, at both private and public universities. We sent these e-mails that were identical, except we varied the race and gender of the name of the applicant.

These e-mails said, "Dear professor so-and-so, I'll be on campus on XYZ day, on a Monday or Tuesday, and was wondering if I could take some time to learn about your research." The names on these e-mails were Chinese names, Indian names, African-American-, Latino- and white-sounding names. We pretested all these names to ensure that they did signal the race and gender we thought they would.

We expected to see more stereotyping or discrimination (i.e., fewer responses) to nonwhite males when asked to meet next week versus today. Why? Today everyone's pretty busy, and so there's no time for the stereotypes or snap judgments to come into your mind about who might be a more qualified student, who you might want to respond to and meet with.

However, in a meeting request for next week, you might go through more scrutiny about whether the candidate is worthy of your time. We thought that's when stereotypes would set in. Maybe for some categories, it's "Do they have English-language proficiency?" For other categories, given the lack of minorities in academia in general, there might be the question of "Can they cut it?"

As we predicted, we did find fewer responses for all of the other categories, relative to the responses to white males, for a meeting request for next week. The question then was whether we'd see this when we matched the race and the gender of the professor with the race and the gender of the student. We still found that requests for next week, regardless of the race of the professor, are lower for candidates other than white males.

As an African-American professor, in the early days of my teaching, I'd often find myself setting up to teach a class, and somebody, usually a prospective student, would come in and say, "I'd like to sit in and learn more about this class. Where's the professor?" They would say that to me as I was setting up, looking like the professor—on the computer, getting everything ready. That, for me, was a perfect example of how stereotypes can play a role.

The stereotype of what a professor looks like—an older white man with gray hair—is one of the factors that might make somebody come in, see a person at the podium preparing for work and wearing a suit, and ask who the professor is. I love those moments, in some ways, because one of the ways in which you change people's stereotypes is by having counter-stereotypical exemplars.

Q: Let's talk more about that. How can we combat stereotypes or try to reduce the harm they cause?

A: I think one of the ways we can reduce the harm of stereotypes is just being aware. Sometimes you'll be walking down the street, and you'll make a snap judgment and not even realize it. But I think one of the critical aspects is noticing, "Oh wow, that came up for me. That's interesting," and thinking, "Where did that come from?" We can change our behavior when we're more aware that our behavior is being influenced by stereotypes.

The other way is by being exposed to counter-stereotypical exemplars. As an African-American, female professor, a student's mere exposure to me means that the next time they go into a classroom with an African-American woman setting up, or someone else who might defy the stereotype of what a professor looks like, they won't automatically say, "Where's the professor?"

I often tell my students they have a beautiful opportunity to be the walking, breathing and living counter-stereotypical exemplars in their work environments. I ask them to think about the stereotypes that exist about them, the stereotypes that exist about people around them, the stereotypes that exist about people on their teams—and to realize that, every day, they have the opportunity to defy those stereotypes.

About the Authors

Katy Milkman is a behavioral scientist and James G. Dinan Professor of Operations, Information and Decisions at the Wharton School at the University of Pennsylvania. She is also author of the book How to Change: The Science of Getting from Where You Are to Where You Want to Be, *host of the podcast Choiceology and co-director of the Behavior Change for Good Initiative. Follow Milkman on Twitter @Katy_Milkman.*

Kassie Brabaw is a journalist writing about health, relationships and astronomy. Find her work at Health, *SELF.com,* Women's Health, *VICE.com and Space.com.*

The Science of Microaggressions: It's Complicated

By Scott Lilienfeld

The story of racial prejudice in the U.S. over the past several decades is a tale of good and bad news. On the mostly positive side, surveys of the American public suggest that overt prejudice–biases to which people are willing to admit–has been on the steady decline (although some data suggest an uptick following the presidential election of Barack Obama). On the negative side, prejudice, even in its ugliest forms, is far from eradicated. In the weeks preceding my writing of this column racial slurs surfaced on the gates of the home of basketball superstar LeBron James, and nooses were found hanging at museums in our nation's capital.

What's more, such overt prejudice might only be the tip of a massive iceberg. A number of prominent scholars have maintained that a good deal of racial bias has merely "gone underground," assuming insidious forms such as implicit prejudice. Although the science of implicit prejudice is controversial, few researchers dispute that bigotry is at times manifested in subtle ways.

Against this backdrop, the concept of "microaggressions" has recently received a flurry of attention. Coined in 1970 by Harvard University psychiatrist Chester Pierce, the term "microggression" refers to a subtle slight or snub directed toward historically stigmatized individuals, especially minorities. The concept lay largely dormant until 2007, when an influential article by Columbia University counseling psychologist Derald Wing Sue and his co-authors brought it to the attention of a mainstream academic audience. According to Sue and his collaborators, the toxicity of microaggressions stems largely from their ambiguity.

Victims of these often largely invisible but pernicious statements and actions find themselves trapped in a catch-22. If they ignore microaggressions directed their way, they risk becoming the target of future transgressions from the same "perpetrators," the term commonly used in the microaggression literature to refer to people who regularly emit such statements and actions. In contrast, if victims accuse perpetrators of aggressing against them, they risk being accused of hypersensitivity and even paranoia.

Sue and co-authors further contend that each microaggression carries a single implicit message. For example, according to them, the microaggression "America is a melting pot" communicates that minority individuals should assimilate into the broader culture, and the microaggression "You are so articulate" communicates that most minority individuals are inarticulate. When encountered frequently over long stretches of time, Sue and colleagues argue, microaggressions exert a detrimental impact on recipients, contributing to low self-esteem and, in some cases, clinical levels of depression, anxiety and other mental health problems.

Over the past few years, the term "microaggression" has become widely used on college and university campuses as well as in scores of businesses. Hundreds of institutions of higher learning now distribute standard lists of microaggressions, many of them modeled after a compendium that appeared in Sue and colleagues' 2007 article, and warn faculty and staff members to steer clear of them.

Many colleges and universities have also instituted training programs to educate faculty staff about the hazards of microaggressions; these programs have caught on in numerous corporations, too. And several Facebook pages are dedicated to the reporting of microaggressions. Not surprisingly, in 2015 the Global Language Monitor dubbed "microaggression" its word of the year.

To be clear, Sue and his collaborators deserve credit for helping to bring the prevalence and importance of subtle prejudice to wider public and academic attention. But is the microaggression concept grounded in solid science, and is it helpful? It is certainly possible microaggressions can in some cases be harmful, especially when people are exposed to them repeatedly for years, and we need to study this phenomenon better so that we can encourage difficult conversations, not squelch them. Nevertheless, given the provisional state of the literature, it is all but impossible to determine the degree to which people's reactions to microaggressions are attributable to these stimuli themselves as opposed to people's subjective reactions to them.

In an article published earlier this year in the Association for Psychological Science journal *Perspectives on Psychological Science*, I canvassed the extant literature to address these questions. In general, I found that the sizable program of research dedicated to microaggressions raises far more questions than answers, and is far too preliminary to justify real-world applications, including training programs.

For one thing, microaggressions as Sue and others conceptualize them lie entirely in the eyes of the beholder. Therefore, if a person feels "microaggressed" against, he or she is automatically deemed to be the victim of a microaggression. The problems here are twofold: First, if person A is offended by a statement but person B is not, this would mean it both is and is not a microaggression, a proposition that is patently illogical. Second, science hinges on the ability to corroborate findings using converging sources of evidence. If a concept is entirely subjective, it is exceedingly difficult to study it scientifically, let alone subject it to rigorous tests.

Further, the very term "microaggression" is fraught, as it implies that the person emitting microaggressions is behaving aggressively. Yet, Sue and his collaborators admit most microaggressions are inadvertent. This acknowledgment leads to another logical contradiction, because psychologists almost invariably define aggression as intentional harm directed toward another person (or animal). The worry here is more than semantic. Psychological research demonstrates that if person A believes that person B's actions are intentionally hostile, he or she is more likely to respond aggressively in turn. People's perceived motives matter.

Like many psychological concepts, microaggression has fuzzy boundaries. That fact by itself is not troubling. Psychologists routinely conduct high-quality research on such concepts as intelligence, impulsivity and depression, none of which lends itself to a strict, dictionary-type (or what scientists call "operational") definition.

Still, the microaggression concept is so nebulously defined that virtually any statement or action that might offend someone could fall within its capacious borders. For example, according to Sue and his colleagues, saying that "America is a land of opportunity" is a microaggression. Yet many nonprejudiced Americans, including many minorities, would surely endorse that assertion. In a study published in a major journal one researcher argued that a clinical supervisor being overly critical of a trainee counts as a microaggression; yet, he or she being insufficiently critical of this same trainee counts as a microaggression, too.

In some cases, the boundaries of the microaggression concept have become so vast as to invite ridicule. Last year an employee forum at the University of North Carolina at Chapel Hill proclaimed that telling a co-worker, "I love your shoes" or organizing golf outings with fellow colleagues were microaggressions (in the first case, because doing so might be perceived as patronizing, in the second case because doing so might be perceived as presumptuous). And a group of researchers recently labeled the phrase "God bless you" following a sneeze as a microaggression, presumably because it might offend certain nonreligious individuals. To his credit, even Sue has expressed misgivings with the increasingly indiscriminate application of the microaggression concept. Yet without considerably greater clarity regarding the definition of microaggressions, misuse and abuse of the concept seems virtually inevitable.

A final key problem is that the microaggression literature neglects to distinguish between the perceived and the perceiver. For decades, psychologists have recognized that our reactions to the world are shaped by both reality and our interpretations of it. Research demonstrates certain people are marked by consistently high levels of hostile attributional bias: a propensity to perceive aggressive intent in response to ambiguous stimuli.

The science aside, it is crucial to ask whether conceptualizing the interpersonal world in terms of microaggressions does more good than harm. The answer is "We don't know." Still, there are reasons for concern. Encouraging individuals to be on the lookout for subtle, in some cases barely discernible, signs of prejudice in others puts just about everyone on the defensive. Minority individuals are likely to become chronically vigilant to minor indications of potential psychological harm whereas majority individuals are likely to feel a need to walk on eggshells, closely monitoring their every word and action to avoid offending others. As a consequence, microaggression training may merely ramp up already simmering racial tensions.

None of this means the microaggression concept is useless. It might be helpful if viewed as the beginning, not as the end, of a constructive and mutually enlightening conversation between two people of differing backgrounds. If instead of saying, "You microaggressed against me. I am offended by your prejudice and you need to stop," people were instead to say, "You probably didn't mean to do so, and perhaps I'm taking this the wrong way, but I was a bit hurt by what you said. Maybe we're just misunderstanding each other. Let's talk," college campuses and businesses would be far better off. We need to encourage difficult conversations, not stifle them.

The views expressed are those of the author(s) and are not necessarily those of Scientific American.

About the Author

Scott Lilienfeld is a professor of psychology at Emory University.

How to Think about 'Implicit Bias'

By Keith Payne, Laura Niemi, John M. Doris

When's the last time a stereotype popped into your mind? If you are like most people, the authors included, it happens all the time. That doesn't make you a racist, sexist or whatever-ist. It means your brain is noticing patterns and making generalizations. But the same thought processes that make people smart can also make them biased. This tendency for stereotype-confirming thoughts to pass spontaneously through our minds is what psychologists call implicit bias. It sets people up to overgeneralize, sometimes leading to discrimination even when people feel they are being fair.

Studies of implicit bias have drawn ire from both the right and the left. For the right, talk of implicit bias is just another instance of progressives seeing injustice under every bush. For the left, implicit bias diverts attention from more damaging instances of explicit bigotry. Debates have become heated and have leaped from scientific journals to the popular press. Along the way, some important points have been lost. We highlight two misunderstandings that anyone who wants to understand implicit bias should know about.

First, much of the controversy centers on the most famous implicit bias test, the Implicit Association Test (IAT). A majority of people taking this test show evidence of implicit bias, suggesting that most individuals are implicitly biased even if they do not think of themselves as prejudiced. As with any measure, the test does have limitations. The stability of the test is low, meaning that if you take the same test a few weeks apart, you might score very differently. And the correlation between a person's IAT scores and discriminatory behavior is often small.

The IAT is a measure, and it doesn't follow from a particular *measure* being flawed that the *phenomenon* we are attempting to measure is not real. Drawing that conclusion is to commit the Divining Rod Fallacy: just because a rod doesn't find water doesn't mean there's no such thing as water. A smarter move is to ask, "What does the other evidence show?"

In fact, there is lots of other evidence. There are perceptual illusions, for example, in which white subjects perceive Black faces as angrier than white faces with the same expression. Bias can cause people to see harmless objects as weapons when they are in the hands of Black men and to dislike abstract images that are paired with Black faces. And there are dozens of variants of laboratory tasks finding that most participants are faster to identify bad words paired with Black faces than with white faces. None of these measures is without limitations, but each shows the same pattern of reliable bias as the IAT. There is a mountain of evidence–independent of any single test–that implicit bias is real.

The second misunderstanding is about what scientists mean when they say a measure predicts behavior. One frequent complaint is that an individual's IAT score doesn't tell you whether the person will discriminate on a particular occasion. This is to commit the Palm Reading Fallacy: unlike palm readers, research psychologists aren't usually in the business of telling you, as an individual, what your life holds in store. Most measures in psychology, from aptitude tests to personality scales, are useful for predicting how *groups* will respond on *average*, not forecasting how particular *individuals* will behave.

The difference is crucial. Knowing that an employee scored high on conscientiousness won't tell you much about whether their work will be careful or sloppy if you inspect it right now. But if a large company hires hundreds of employees who are all conscientious, this will likely pay off with a small but consistent increase in careful work on average.

Implicit bias researchers have always warned against using the tests for predicting individual outcomes, such as how a particular manager will behave in job interviews–they've never been in the palm-reading business. What the IAT does, and does well, is predict average outcomes across larger entities such as counties, cities or states. For example, metro areas with greater average implicit bias have larger racial disparities in police shootings. And counties with greater average implicit bias have larger racial disparities in infant health problems. These correlations are important: the lives of Black citizens and newborn Black babies depend on them.

Field experiments demonstrate that real-world discrimination continues and is widespread. White applicants get about 50 percent more callbacks than Black applicants with the same résumés; college professors are 26 percent more likely to respond to a student's e-mail when it is signed by Brad rather than Lamar; and physicians recommend less pain medication for Black patients than for white patients with the same injury.

Today managers are unlikely to announce that white job applicants should be chosen over Black applicants, and physicians don't declare that Black people feel less pain than white people. Yet the broad pattern of discrimination and disparities seen in field studies persists. It bears a much closer resemblance to the widespread stereotypical thoughts seen on implicit bias tests than to results of survey studies in which most people present themselves as unbiased.

One reason people on both the right and the left are skeptical of implicit bias might be pretty simple: it isn't nice to think we aren't very nice. It would be comforting to conclude, when we don't consciously entertain impure intentions, that all of our intentions are pure. Unfortunately, we can't conclude that: many of us are more biased than we realize. And that is an important cause of injustice—whether you know it or not.

Referenced

Physicians and Implicit Bias: How Doctors May Unwittingly Perpetuate Health Care Disparities. Elizabeth N. Chapman, Anna Kaatz and Molly Carnes in *Journal of General Internal Medicine*, Vol. 28, No. 11, pages 1504–1510; November 2013.

Condoning Stereotyping? How Awareness of Stereotyping Prevalence Impacts Expression of Stereotypes. Michelle M. Duguid and Melissa C. Thomas-Hunt in *Journal of Applied Psychology*, Vol. 100, No. 2, pages 343–359; March 2015.

About the Authors

Keith Payne is a professor in psychology and neuroscience at the University of North Carolina at Chapel Hill. He is author of The Broken Ladder: How Inequality Affects the Way We Think, Live, and Die *(Viking, 2017).*

Laura Niemi is an assistant professor in the department of psychology at Cornell University. She researches moral judgment and the implications of differences in moral values.

John M. Doris is Peter L. Dyson Professor of Ethics in Organizations and Life at the Charles H. Dyson School of Applied Economics and Management and a professor at the Sage School of Philosophy at Cornell University.

The Flexibility of Racial Bias

By Mina Cikara, Jay Van Bavel

In 2013 the Black Lives Matter movement began after George Zimmerman was acquitted for shooting Trayvon Martin, a 17-year-old Black teen. The following year the movement triggered national protests after the killing of Michael Brown and Eric Garner. In 2020 the murders of Breonna Taylor and George Floyd led to global protests against racial injustice. These are not isolated incidents. Institutional and systemic racism reinforce discrimination in countless situations, including hiring, sentencing, housing and mortgage lending.

It would be easy to see in all this powerful evidence that racism is a permanent fixture in America's social fabric and even, perhaps, an inevitable aspect of human nature. Indeed, the mere act of labeling others according to their age, gender or race is a reflexive habit of the human mind. Social groupings such as race that we have come to think of as "categories" influence our thinking quickly, often outside of our awareness. Extensive research has found that these implicit racial biases–subconscious negative thoughts and feelings about people from other races–are automatic, pervasive and difficult to suppress. Neuroscientists have explored racial prejudice by exposing people to images of faces while scanning their brains in functional MRI machines. Early studies found that when people viewed faces of another race, the amount of activity in the amygdala–a small brain structure associated with experiencing emotions, including fear–was associated with individual differences on measures of implicit racial bias.

This work has led many to conclude that racial biases might be part of a primitive–and possibly hardwired–neural fear response to racial out-groups. These results, coupled with pervasive discrimination and ongoing violence, paint a bleak picture. But scientists have learned that the amygdala's role in implicit bias is more complex than it first seemed. Moreover, recent findings from psychology and neuroscience have found that individual prejudices and their neural underpinnings are surprisingly flexible. It seems that the key factor in predicting our responses to other groups is not simply their race but rather whether we believe "they" are with us or against us. Group allegiances can turn on a dime, in some cases effectively "erasing race" from people's judgments or creating new classes of enemies (for example, the increase in anti-Muslim hate crimes after 9/11). This new evidence of the flexibility of implicit bias illustrates that we are not hardwired to be racist—and, furthermore, that prejudice can be reduced under the right conditions.

There is little question that categories such as race, gender, age, and other social categories play a major role in shaping the biases and stereotypes that people bring to bear in their judgments of others. But research has found that how people categorize themselves may be just as fundamental to understanding prejudice as how they categorize others. When people categorize themselves as part of a group, their self-concept shifts from the individual ("I") to the collective level ("us"). People form groups rapidly and favor members of their own group even when groups are formed on arbitrary grounds, such as the simple flip of a coin. These findings highlight the remarkable ease with which humans form *coalitions*. And this seems to be a universal human tendency—every culture ever studied displays this same propensity.

Many studies have shown that coalition-based preferences override race-based preferences. For instance, our research has revealed that the simple act of placing people on a mixed-race team can diminish their automatic racial bias. In a series of experiments, white participants who were randomly placed on a mixed-race team—the Tigers or Lions—showed little evidence of implicit racial bias. Merely belonging to a mixed-race team triggered positive automatic associations with all the members of their own group, regardless of race. Being part of one of these seemingly trivial mixed-race groups produced similar effects on brain activity—the amygdala responded to team membership rather than race.

The same dynamic is at play in politics. For example, both Democrats and Republicans in the U.S. favor the resumes of those affiliated with their political party much more than they favor those who share their race. These coalition-based preferences remain powerful even in the absence of the animosity present in electoral politics. Taken together, these studies indicate that momentary changes in group membership can override the influence of race on the way we see, think about and feel toward people who are different from ourselves.

Although these coalition-based distinctions might be the most basic building block of bias, they say little about the other factors that cause group conflict. Why do some groups get ignored while others get attacked? Whenever we encounter a new person or group, we are motivated to answer two questions as quickly as possible: Is this person a friend or foe, and are they capable of enacting their intentions toward me? In other words, once we have determined that someone is a member of an out-group, we need to determine what kind. The nature of the relations between groups—Are they cooperative or competitive, or neither?—and their relative status—Do they have access to resources?—largely determine the course of intergroup interactions.

Groups that are seen as competitive with one's interests, and capable of enacting their opposing intentions, are much more likely to be targets of hostility than more benevolent (elderly) or powerless (homeless) groups. This is one reason why sports rivalries have such psychological potency. For instance, fans of the Boston Red Sox are more likely to feel pleasure, and exhibit reward-related neural responses, at the misfortunes of the archrival New York Yankees than other baseball teams (and vice versa)—especially in the midst of a tight playoff race. (How much fans take pleasure in the misfortunes of their rivals is also linked to how likely they would be to harm fans from the other team.)

Just as a particular person's group membership can be flexible, so, too, are the relations between groups. Groups that have previously had cordial relations may become rivals (and vice versa). Indeed, psychological and biological responses to out-group members can change, depending on whether or not that out-group is perceived as threatening. For example, people exhibit greater pleasure—they smile—in response to the misfortunes of stereotypically competitive groups (investment bankers); however, this malicious pleasure is reduced when you provide participants with counterstereotypic information (investment bankers who are working with small companies to help them weather an economic downturn). Competition between "us" and "them" can even distort our judgments of distance, making threatening out-groups seem much closer than they really are. These distorted perceptions can serve to amplify intergroup discrimination: the more different and distant "they" are, the easier it is to disrespect and harm them.

Thus, not all out-groups are treated the same: some elicit indifference, whereas others become targets of antipathy. Stereotypically threatening groups are especially likely to be targeted with violence, but those stereotypes can be tempered with other information. If perceptions of intergroup relations can be changed, individuals may overcome hostility toward perceived foes and become more responsive to one another's grievances.

The flexible nature of both group membership and intergroup relations offers reason to be cautiously optimistic about the potential for greater cooperation among groups in conflict (be they Black versus white or citizens versus police). One strategy is to bring multiple groups together around a common goal. For example, in an experiment conducted during the fiercely contested 2008 Democratic presidential primary process, Hillary Clinton and Barack Obama supporters gave more money to strangers who supported the same primary candidate (compared with the rival candidate). Two months later, after the Democratic National Convention, the supporters of both candidates coalesced around the party nominee–Barack Obama–and this bias disappeared.

We have found that creating a sense of cohesion between competitive groups can increase empathy for the suffering of our rivals. These strategies can help reduce aggression toward out-groups, which is critical for creating more chances for constructive dialogue addressing greater social injustices.

Of course, instilling a sense of common identity and cooperation is extremely difficult in entrenched intergroup conflicts, but when it happens, the benefits are obvious. Consider how the community leaders in New York City and in Ferguson, Mo., responded differently to protests against police brutality—in N.Y.C., political leaders expressed grief and concern over police brutality and moved quickly to make policy changes in policing, whereas the leaders and police in Ferguson suppressed protests with high-tech military vehicles and riot gear. In the first case, groups came together with a common goal—to increase the safety of everyone in the community; in the latter, the actions of the police likely reinforced the "us" and "them" distinctions and amplified discord.

Tragically, these types of conflicts continue to roil the country. And the fact that our modern stereotypes and prejudices are tightly linked to historical mistreatment and oppression makes it very hard to find sustainable solutions to these problems. Understanding the psychology and neuroscience of social identity and intergroup relations cannot undo the effects of systemic racism and discriminatory practices; however, it can offer insights into the psychological processes responsible for escalating—or de-escalating—the tension between, for example, civilians and police officers.

Even in cases where it isn't possible to create a common identity among groups in conflict, it may be possible to blur the boundaries between groups. In one recent experiment, we sorted participants into groups—red versus blue—competing for a cash prize. Half of the participants were randomly assigned to see a picture of a segregated social network of all the players, in which red dots clustered together, blue dots clustered together, and the two clusters were separated by white space. The other half of the participants saw an integrated social network in which the red and blue dots were mixed together in one large cluster. Participants who thought the two teams were interconnected with one another reported greater empathy for the out-group players compared with those who had seen the segregated network. Thus, reminding people that individuals could be connected to one another despite being from different groups may be another way to build trust and understanding among them.

A mere month before Freddie Gray died in Baltimore in police custody, President Obama addressed the nation on the 50th anniversary of Bloody Sunday in Selma: "We do a disservice to the cause of justice by intimating that bias and discrimination are immutable or that racial division is inherent to America. To deny ... progress—our progress—would be to rob us of our own agency; our responsibility to do what we can to make America better."

Research from psychology and neuroscience indicates that we, as individuals, possess this capacity. Understanding this fact means that we have a responsibility to reduce prejudice and discrimination. Of course, reducing prejudice is not sufficient to usher in racial equality or peace. Even when the level of prejudice against particular out-groups decreases, it does not imply that the level of institutional discrimination against these or other groups will necessarily improve. In many cases, even egalitarian people can perpetuate harm if the systems in place are already unjust.

Ultimately only collective action and institutional evolution can address systemic racism. The science, however, is clear on one thing: individual bias and discrimination are changeable. Race-based prejudice and discrimination, in particular, are created and reinforced by many social factors, but they are not inevitable consequences of our biology. We hope that understanding how coalitional thinking impacts intergroup relations will make it easier for us to affect real social change going forward.

About the Authors

Mina Cikara is an assistant professor of psychology and director of the Intergroup Neuroscience Lab at Harvard University. Her research examines the conditions under which groups and individuals are denied social value, agency and empathy. Cikara tweets about psychology and neuroscience at @profcikara.

Jay Van Bavel is an assistant professor of psychology and director of the Social Identity and Morality Laboratory at New York University. He studies how our collective concerns—group identities, moral values and political beliefs—alter our perceptions and evaluations of the world around us.

The Problem with Implicit Bias Training

By Tiffany L. Green, Nao Hagiwara

While the nation roils with ongoing protests against police violence and persistent societal racism, many organizations have released statements promising to do better. These promises often include improvements to hiring practices; a priority on retaining and promoting people of color; and pledges to better serve those people as customers and clients.

As these organizations work to make good on their declarations, implicit bias training is often at the top of the list. As the thinking goes, these nonconscious prejudices and stereotypes are spontaneously and automatically activated and may inadvertently affect how white Americans see and treat Black people and other people of color. The hope is that, with proper training, people can learn to recognize and correct this damaging form of bias.

In the health care industry, implicit bias is among the likely culprits in many persistent racial and ethnic disparities, like infant and maternal mortality, chronic diseases such as diabetes, and more recently, COVID-19. Black Americans are about 2.5 times more likely to die from COVID-19 relative to whites, and emerging data indicate that Native Americans are also disproportionately suffering from the pandemic. Implicit biases may impact the ways in which clinicians and other health care professionals diagnose and treat people of color, leading to worse outcomes. In response to these disparities, Michigan and California have mandated implicit bias training for some health professionals.

There's just one problem. We just don't have the evidence yet that implicit bias training actually works.

To be sure, finding ways to counter unfair treatment is critical. The evidence is clear that implicit prejudice, an affective component of implicit bias (i.e., feeling or emotion) exists among health care providers with respect to Black and/or Latinx patients, as well as to dark-skinned patients not in those categories. In turn, these biases lower the quality of patient-provider communication and result in lower satisfaction with the healthcare encounter.

But while implicit bias trainings are multiplying, few rigorous evaluations of these programs exist. There are exceptions; some implicit bias interventions have been conducted empirically among health care professionals and college students. These interventions have been proven to lower scores on the Implicit Association Test (IAT), the most commonly used implicit measure of prejudice and stereotyping. But to date, none of these interventions has been shown to result in permanent, long-term reductions of implicit bias scores or, more importantly, sustained and meaningful changes in behavior (i.e., narrowing of racial/ethnic clinical treatment disparities).

Even worse, there is consistent evidence that bias training done the "wrong way" (think lukewarm diversity training) can actually have the opposite impact, inducing anger and frustration among white employees. What this all means is that, despite the widespread calls for implicit bias training, it will likely be ineffective at best; at worst, it's a poor use of limited resources that could cause more damage and exacerbate the very issues it is trying to solve.

So, what should we do? The first thing is to realize that racism is not just an individual problem requiring an individual intervention, but a structural and organizational problem that will require a lot of work to change. It's much easier for organizations to offer an implicit bias training than to take a long, hard look and overhaul the way they operate. The reality is, even if we could reliably reduce individual-level bias, various forms of institutional racism embedded in health care (and other organizations) would likely make these improvements hard to maintain.

Explicit, uncritical racial stereotyping in medicine is one good example. We have known for many years that race is a social construct rather than a proxy for genetic or biological differences. Even so, recent work has identified numerous cases of race-adjusted clinical algorithms in medicine. In nephrology, for example, race adjustments that make it appear as if Black patients have better kidney function than they actually do can potentially lead to worse outcomes such as delays in referral for needed specialist care or kidney transplantation. Other more insidious stereotyping characterizes Native Americans and African Americans as more likely to be "noncompliant" with diet and lifestyle advice. These characterizations of noncompliance as a function of attitudes and practices completely ignore structural factors such as poverty, segregation and marketing–factors that create health inequities in the first place.

Meaningful progress at the structural and institutional levels takes longer than a few days of implicit bias training. But there are encouraging examples of individuals who have fought successfully for structural change within their health care organizations. For example, medical students at the University of Washington successfully lobbied for race to be removed as a criterion for determining kidney function–a process that took many years. Their success may have important implications for closing gaps in disparities among patients with renal disease. And innovative new programs like the Mid-Ohio Farmacy have linked health care providers with community-based organizations, and help providers address food insecurity among their low-income patients–an issue that disproportionately impacts people of color. (Doctors can write a "food prescription" that allows their patients to purchase fresh produce.)

None of this, of course, means that we should give up on trying to understand implicit bias or developing evidence-based training that successfully reduces discriminatory behaviors at the individual level. What it does mean is that we need to lean into the hard work of auditing long-standing practices that unfairly stigmatize people of color and fail to take into account how health inequities evolve. Creating organizations that value equity and ultimately produce better outcomes for people of color will be long, hard work, but it's necessary and it's been a long time coming.

About the Authors

Tiffany L. Green, Ph.D. is an assistant professor in the Department of Population Health Sciences and the Department of Obstetrics and Gynecology at the University of Wisconsin-Madison.

Nao Hagiwara, Ph.D., is an associate professor in the Department of Psychology at Virginia Commonwealth University.

To Fight Bias, Consider Highlighting Your Race or Gender

By Erika Kirgios, Aneesh Rai, Edward Chang, Katy Milkman

A friend (let's call her Rosa) recently spent several weeks cold-e-mailing business school alumni who had built successful ventures. Rosa is a woman of color and an aspiring entrepreneur, and she planned to apply to business school herself. She hoped to build her network or at least get some useful advice. But she faced a dilemma: In her messages, should she highlight that she's a woman and a member of a racial minority group in entrepreneurship–or let her identity fade into the background?

We were also curious. After all, Rosa's identity might help her stand out in a positive way, or it could trigger a prejudiced response. So we decided to do some research. We surveyed 200 people who identified as women or members of racial or ethnic minority groups to ask what they would do in Rosa's shoes. Only 35 percent told us they would highlight their identity in requests for career support. Rosa herself, who ultimately decided not to mention her identity, articulated a concern that many of our respondents shared: "I'm worried I'll come off as needy or seeking attention or like I'm playing this 'race' or 'female' card if I mention my identity explicitly."

These fears are reasonable. Several decades of experiments have shown that women and members of racial minority groups whose name signals their identity typically receive fewer responses than white men to otherwise identical e-mails or job applications. Just signing an e-mail as "Amanda Cabot," "Alma Hernandez" or "Deshawn Washington" leads people to assume that they know your race, ethnicity or gender. If the signature alone makes someone less likely to respond to a message, it's sensible to worry that drawing *extra* attention to your marginalized identity can only make things worse.

But our recent research suggests the opposite is often true. We have found that explicitly mentioning your underrepresented identity when seeking career help can be *beneficial*.

We first tested this idea in a large experiment with local elected officials. We sent networking e-mails to 2,476 white, male city councilmen from 701 U.S. cities, including giant ones such as New York City and smaller ones such as Bentonville, Ark. Our e-mails appeared to come from students who said they wanted advice about going into politics. (In reality, these students were fictitious.) We varied the senders, using names that suggested they were white men (e.g., "Hunter Anderson"), white women (e.g., "Abigail Miller"), Black men (e.g., "Tyrone Robinson"), Black women (e.g., "Aliyah Harris"), Latinos (e.g., "Alejandro Gutierrez") or Latinas (e.g., "Camila Rodriguez"). All the e-mails were identical except that some messages explicitly mentioned the fictional sender's identity and others did not.

We sent our e-mails on a Tuesday morning. Within one week, about a third of the contacted politicians had replied. Response rates to e-mails from names perceived as belonging to white men were similar, whether they referred to themselves as a "young person" or referenced their gender by describing themselves as a "young man." (We did not use e-mails that directly referred to white senders' racial identity because preliminary tests suggested that recipients would associate such messages with white nationalism.)

Things got more interesting when we analyzed responses to messages from women and racial or ethnic minority group members. When female or minority senders explicitly mentioned their identities, they were just more than 24 percent more likely to receive a response, compared with e-mails that had the same signature but did not mention identities. E-mails that mentioned identities received higher-quality replies, too: politicians wrote responses that were about 32 percent longer and about 39 percent more likely to offer to set up a phone call or meeting.

Strikingly, mentioning identity had the biggest benefit for Black men. Politicians were about 60 percent more likely to respond to messages from Black men when they asked councilmen to write back with "a few words of wisdom for a young Black man hoping to one day become a city councilor, like you." This effect held regardless of the politicians' ideological leaning or proximity to reelection. Moreover mentioning identity was just as likely to benefit women and members of racial or ethnic minority groups in cities that voted for Donald Trump in 2016 as in cities that voted for Hillary Clinton. And the effect persisted regardless of the city's size, demographic diversity or wealth.

These effects extend beyond politicians. In another experiment, we sent 1,169 undergraduates at an Ivy League university an e-mail from a (fictitious) Black, male graduate student named Demarcus Rivers, who asked for help with his dissertation research. Regardless of the recipients' gender, race or political leaning, when Demarcus described himself as "a Black man working towards a Ph.D.," students were almost twice as likely to volunteer to help him.

Why is it so important to mention that you're "a woman in STEM" or "a Black man pursuing a law degree"? Our research suggests that drawing attention to your marginalized identity or minority status reminds people on the receiving end of your message that bias could influence their decision-making. That reminder, in turn, may motivate them to monitor their own reaction more closely and behave more helpfully. Most Americans want to avoid appearing or feeling prejudiced, whether that avoidance is to uphold their values or reputation. Helping someone who explicitly identifies as part of an underrepresented or disadvantaged community feels like an opportunity to prove to yourself or others that you support women and racial and ethnic minority groups and are therefore not prejudiced. A rosy read of our results would be that people just need a little nudge to behave in line with their values.

But prejudice exists, and it does have negative effects on people's professional lives. Work by other researchers suggests that women and members of racial minority groups whose name or curriculum vitae gives away their identity can benefit from hiding their gender or race when they are evaluated for a job. For example, one study found that Asian applicants fared better in U.S. job searches when they "Americanized" their name and interests, changing their name from "Lei" to "Luke," for example, or citing popular Western hobbies such as snowboarding.

This finding might seem to contradict our research. But a more accurate interpretation is that these studies all point to the dangers of allowing one's name alone to convey identity. Because sexism, racism and other forms of bias are all too common in the workplace, a signature that *leaks* your identity can trigger stereotypes that lead to discriminatory behavior. Concealing your identity can block the stereotyping process before it begins. Our work, meanwhile, offers another strategy to address the same problem. By highlighting your identity, you can prompt people to actively identify and suppress their potentially prejudiced responses.

The onus of reducing discrimination should not be on women and people of color. But in a world where inequity and bias are commonplace, having a tool to blunt these barriers may come in handy.

About the Authors

Erika Kirgios is a doctoral candidate in the operations, information and decisions department at the Wharton School at the University of Pennsylvania. She studies the decision-making biases that underlie inequality and designs interventions to improve outcomes for women and members of racial and ethnic minority groups. Follow Kirgios on Twitter @erika_kirgios.

Aneesh Rai is a doctoral candidate in the operations, information and decisions department at the Wharton School at the University of Pennsylvania. He researches factors that contribute to a lack of diversity in organizations, as well as interventions to help organizations become more diverse. Follow Rai on Twitter @aneeshrai17.

Edward Chang is an assistant professor of negotiation, organizations and markets at Harvard Business School. He researches evidence-based solutions to increase diversity, equity and inclusion in organizations.

Katy Milkman is a behavioral scientist and James G. Dinan Professor of Operations, Information and Decisions at the Wharton School at the University of Pennsylvania. She is also author of the book How to Change: The Science of Getting from Where You Are to Where You Want to Be, *host of the podcast Choiceology and co-director of the Behavior Change for Good Initiative. Follow Milkman on Twitter @Katy_Milkman.*

Section 2: Understanding Gender and Sexuality through Science

Doctors Must Dig into Gender Difference to Improve Women's Health Care

By Marcia L. Stefanick

In January 2013 the U.S. Food and Drug Administration cut the recommended dose of the nation's most popular sleep drug, Ambien, in half for women but not for men. The FDA had determined that 15 percent of the 5.7 million women using zolpidem products (the active ingredient in Ambien) were experiencing driving impairment eight hours after taking the drug, compared with 3 percent of the 3.5 million male zolpidem users.

Researchers had known for a long time that women, on average, clear zolpidem from their body much more slowly than men do. Indeed, drug metabolism, tolerance, side effects and benefits differ significantly between the average man and woman for many widely prescribed medications, with women having a 50 to 70 percent higher chance of an adverse reaction. Body size, proportion of fat to muscle and a host of other factors, including hormonal influences, account for these differences. But physicians rarely consider these dynamics when writing prescriptions. Ambien, which now comes in bottles with pink (low dose) and blue (original dose) labels, is a rare example of a "sex-specific" medical recommendation. (The FDA now recommends that men also be started on the low dose of the drug, and doctors can use their discretion to increase the dose.)

Drug-dosing problems are just one example of how the health-care system is blind to biological sex differences. As a result, women are too often treated like men. Moreover, the system can be blind to gender bias; some disorders are considered "men's" or "women's," even when both sexes suffer from them. Doctors often fail to diagnose stereotypical "male" conditions in women, and vice versa, until the condition has become dangerous.

These problems arise from a serious gap in our understanding of sex differences. The vast majority of animal research has been conducted only on males, mostly on rodents. And women have been grossly underrepresented in human clinical trials. Even when both sexes are included, sex-specific analyses are generally not reported—and because most subjects are men, the findings may not pertain to women. A 2019 study found that only 7 percent of reports on adverse drug reactions in people with heart failure gave data separately for women and men. And nearly half of these showed significant differences between the two. Not surprisingly, no one understood why a young woman hospitalized with a heart attack was twice as likely to die as a young man. Failure to include women in biomedical research was exacerbated by 1977 FDA guidelines that barred women of childbearing potential from participating in phase I (safety) and phase II (efficacy) trials, whether they were planning a pregnancy or not. Although the FDA now allows for inclusion of pregnant women in research that does not threaten pregnancy, few drugs are approved for pregnant women because safety and effectiveness data are not available.

Fixing the Problem

Changes in practices have been long in coming. In 1990 scientists, advocates and members of Congress pushed the National Institutes of Health to establish the Office of Research on Women's Health. In 1991 cardiologist Bernadine Healy, the first and only woman director of the NIH, launched the Women's Health Initiative, which enrolled nearly 162,000 women across the U.S. The study led to important changes in clinical care; without it, for example, physicians might still believe they should put most older women on hormone therapy, leading to many more heart attacks and strokes and cases of breast cancer. The 1993 NIH Revitalization Act required enrollment of female (and minority) participants in federally supported phase III trials—those designed to determine how a new treatment works in a large group. The act did not, however, require enrollment of enough women to determine how a given treatment affected women specifically.

More change came in 2001, when a landmark Institute of Medicine (IOM) report emphasized the important role that "sex" played in the basic biology that underpins health care. It concluded that "every cell has a sex." Yet almost no cell biologists consider, or even know, the sex of the cells or tissues they study. Nor do they address how sex chromosomes affect the systems they are investigating. The IOM report defined sex as a biological quality or classification of sexually reproducing organisms, generally male or female, derived from chromosomes and sex hormones. Gender was defined, in human studies, as sociocultural–a person's "self-representation as male or female."

This concept can be expanded to include gender norms (social expectations of "masculine" and "feminine" behaviors) and gender relations (how people react to one another because of gender), all of which can exert powerful influences on biology. For example, men are generally stronger than women not only because of biological factors such as larger muscles but also because of gender roles: in many societies, men lift and carry most of the heavy objects. Another example might be the twofold greater incidence of (unipolar) depression in women, which may result from an interaction of biological and social factors, such as women being more likely to be sexually assaulted.

Since the IOM report, scientists, academicians and health policy advocates have been urging their institutions, journals and government agencies to confront the need to include women and female animals in research and to study sex differences. In 2009 the Gendered Innovations project at Stanford University engaged collaborators across the U.S., Canada and the European Union to develop practical methods for sex and gender analysis and to track progress on including sex and gender in research. In 2010 the Office of Research on Women's Health issued a strategic plan that identified the need to integrate sex and gender perspectives in basic science and medical research.

That same year the Canadian Institutes of Health Research went further and began asking grant applicants to indicate whether sex or gender was accounted for in their study proposals. A May 2014 notice in the journal *Nature*, written by Francis Collins, who was then director of the NIH, and Janine Clayton, director of the Office of Research on Women's Health, unveiled policies designed to ensure that NIH-funded preclinical research consider both females and males, as well as the sex of cells. And in January 2016 the NIH began to require that sex as a biological variable be factored into research designs, analyses and reporting. If grant applicants propose to study only one sex, they must present persuasive justification for doing so. In contrast to the Canadian Institutes, however, the NIH did not address the influence of gender on biology.

A Man's Disease

Gender biases profoundly influence diagnoses and treatments and therefore health outcomes. Despite years of "Red Dress" campaigns, most people and many physicians still think of heart disease as a man's disease. They are surprised to learn that heart disease is the number-one killer of U.S. women, far exceeding deaths from breast cancer. Younger women, in particular, often go undiagnosed because physicians do not consider the possibility. Furthermore, women commonly report a range of symptoms beyond chest pain—the key complaint of men—including back pain, nausea, headache, dizziness and pain down the right arm (not just the left). Physicians often refer to these common symptoms as "atypical" because men do not report them.

In addition, although men and older women are likely to have a blockage in one or more of the coronary arteries from localized plaque—a buildup of cholesterol, fat and other substances—younger women are more likely to have diffuse plaque that lines and narrows the entire artery, resulting in inadequate blood supply to the heart. Because no specific blockage is detected, they may be diagnosed as "free of heart disease" yet at high risk of a fatal heart attack. Although newer diagnostic tests can detect this nonobstructive disease, a physician has to consider the possibility that a young woman has heart disease to order them. Prevention and treatment guidelines for women are still based predominantly on male data, despite growing evidence of sex differences in risks and treatment outcomes.

Pregnancy, now recognized as a major cardiovascular stress test, also contributes to sex disparities, yet researchers have only recently begun to realize the serious long-term consequences. Pregnancy-related hypertension and preeclampsia, as well as gestational diabetes (high blood glucose developed during pregnancy), increase a woman's chance of developing subsequent cardiovascular disease nearly twofold, as well as her risk of developing type II diabetes.

Hard to Decipher

Sex differences and gender biases influence medical diagnoses and treatments for *everyone*. Osteoporosis, characterized by reduced bone strength, is considered a woman's disease because white women have twice the lifetime risk of fracturing a bone, compared with white men. Fracture-prevention trials have included few men. Yet men account for nearly one in three hip fractures, and their medical outcomes are worse after the injury.

Men are more susceptible to viral, bacterial, parasitic and fungal infections than women are, although women have greater rates of sexually transmitted infections such as HIV and herpes simplex virus 2. On the other hand, the more robust immune system of women may explain why they constitute more than 70 percent of the 24 million Americans with autoimmune diseases, in which the immune system attacks one's own body tissues. Pregnancy may play a role here as well. Some fetal cells cross into the mother's blood and are found in her circulation decades later, and they have been implicated in some autoimmune diseases.

Sex and gender also shape neurological and mental diseases. Accumulating evidence suggests that the placenta of the male fetus responds to environmental stressors by promoting fetal growth, whereas the female placenta promotes gene and protein expression that increases chances of survival. This difference may contribute to developmental disorders that are diagnosed more often in boys, such as autism and dyslexia–although diagnostic methods may overlook girls.

Gender bias surrounding mental illnesses seems to be widespread. The suggestion that boys and men manifest depression with anger, rather than withdrawal, may arise from a biased expectation that males externalize behaviors and females internalize them. Some mental health professionals around the world still assign certain symptoms almost exclusively to women, such as being "hysterical," whereas men are likely to be diagnosed as "antisocial." These biases affect treatments and health outcomes. In addition, a woman is much more likely to be diagnosed with depression than a man with identical presentation because of gender biases in the medical system. Women also receive more antidepressants and less adequate pain medication when reporting pain because of an incorrect belief that they have a greater tolerance to it. In fact, they have a lower threshold for almost every kind of pain investigated.

Bias is rampant when it comes to the brain. Pop psychology loves the idea that men and women have different brains. Reports show that males have more cortical connections within each of the brain's two hemispheres, whereas women have more connections between the hemispheres. But the reports fail to mention that 86 to 88 percent of all these combined connections are similar–suggesting that male and female brains are more alike than different. Research also increasingly shows that any individual's brain development over a person's lifetime is greatly influenced by neuroplasticity–the ability of brain cells to rewire over time. If the daily experiences of boys and men differ markedly from those of girls and women, differences in brain structure and function should be expected.

This complicated picture makes it difficult to pin down causes and treatments for brain illnesses. Almost two thirds of the more than six million Americans who have Alzheimer's disease are women, not only because more women than men survive to age 65 but also because more women acquire the disease across all age groups.

Time to Get Personal

Clearly, medical researchers and physicians have a lot of untangling to do before they can offer better health care to women. A deeper understanding of sex differences will improve health directives for men, too. In 2015 the NIH launched a Precision Medicine Initiative to address the problem that most treatments have been designed for the "average patient" instead of different individuals. "Precision" or "personalized" medicine is expected to take into account variability in genes, environment and lifestyle for each person. Yet genome-wide studies that try to pinpoint genetic variants that may be linked to specific diseases have generally excluded X and Y chromosomes, suggesting that sex is not an important focus of precision medicine.

In 2015 the Canadian Institutes of Health Research rolled out an online training course on sex and gender in health research, and the League of European Research Universities released a report on how to integrate sex and gender into research processes. In 2016 the NIH mandated that researchers consider sex as a biological variable in animal and human studies, and a panel of 13 experts representing nine countries developed the Sex and Gender Equity in Research guidelines, a comprehensive procedure for reporting sex and gender information in study design, data analyses, results and interpretation of findings. Despite the initiation in 2015 of U.S. educational summits calling for integrating sex- and gender-based evidence into medicine and education, relatively little progress has been made. Several summits have been held to assess any new developments–the latest was held virtually in November 2021. Advancing understanding of sex and gender differences in health and disease and integrating those perspectives into emerging basic science fields and in translational research and technologies are two of the key themes of the NIH report on women's health research.

We might need further mandates, through policy and funding restrictions, to ensure that female biology makes it into textbooks and testing protocols. We might also need to require best practices–standards of care that must be adhered to as part of the ethical code of "do no harm"–to ensure that clinicians and health-care providers consider both sex and gender in medical diagnoses, screening and treatments. Both women and men would benefit enormously. Without sex and gender as a focus, physicians cannot achieve the precision medicine, specific to each of us, that we all hope to receive.

Referenced

Exploring the Biological Contributions to Human Health: Does Sex Matter? Institute of Medicine. National Academies Press, 2001.

Gendered Research and Innovation: Integrating Sex and Gender Analysis into the Research Process. League of European Research Universities, September 2015.

Gendered Innovations project, Stanford University: http://genderedinnovations.stanford.edu

About the Author

Marcia L. Stefanick is a professor of medicine at the Stanford Prevention Research Center and a professor of obstetrics and gynecology at the Stanford University School of Medicine. She is also director of the Stanford Women and Sex Differences in Medicine Center and is conducting a large trial of older women related to heart disease prevention and healthy aging.

Is There a "Female" Brain?

By Lydia Denworth

In 2009 Daphna Joel, a neuroscientist at Tel Aviv University, decided to teach a course on the psychology of gender. As a feminist, she had long been interested in questions of sex and gender, but as a scientist, her research had been mostly on the neural underpinnings of obsessive-compulsive behavior. To prepare for the class, Joel spent a year reviewing much of the extensive and polarized literature on sex differences in the brain. The hundreds of papers covered everything from variations in the size of specific anatomical structures in rats to the possible roots of male aggression and female empathy in humans. At the outset, Joel shared a popularly held assumption: just as sex differences nearly always produce two different reproductive systems, they would also produce two different forms of brains—one female, the other male.

As she continued reading, Joel came across a paper contradicting that idea. The study, published in 2001 by Tracey Shors and her colleagues at Rutgers University, concerned a detail of the rat brain: tiny protrusions on brain cells, called dendritic spines, that regulate transmission of electrical signals. The researchers showed that when estrogen levels were elevated, female rats had more dendritic spines than males did. Shors also found that when male and female rats were subjected to the acutely stressful event of having their tail shocked, their brain responded in opposite ways: males grew more spines; females ended up with fewer.

From this unexpected finding, Joel developed a hypothesis about sex differences in the brain that has stirred up new controversy in a field already steeped in it. Instead of contemplating brain areas that differ between females and males, she suggested that we should consider our brain as a "mosaic" (repurposing a term that had been used by others), arranged from an assortment of variable, sometimes changeable, masculine and feminine features. That variability itself and the behavioral overlap between the sexes—aggressive females and empathetic males and even men and women who display both traits—suggest that brains cannot be lumped into one of two distinct, or dimorphic, categories. That three-pound mass lodged underneath the skull is neither male nor female, Joel says. With her colleagues at Tel Aviv, the Max Planck Institute for Human Cognitive and Brain Sciences in Leipzig, Germany, and the University of Zurich, Joel tested her idea by analyzing MRI brain scans of more than 1,400 brains and demonstrated that most of them did indeed contain both masculine and feminine characteristics. "We all belong to a single, highly heterogeneous population," she says.

When Joel's work was published in 2015 in the *Proceedings of the National Academy of Sciences USA*, like-minded scientists hailed it as a breakthrough. "The result is a major challenge to the entrenched misconceptions," wrote Gina Rippon, a professor of cognitive neuroimaging at Aston University in England. "My hope is it will be a game-changer for the 21st century."

Longtime sex-difference researchers, meanwhile, disagreed strenuously, taking issue with Joel's methodology and conclusions, as well as her overt feminism. "The paper is ideology masquerading as science," says neurobiologist Larry Cahill of the University of California, Irvine, who argues that Joel's statistical methods were "rigged" (albeit not necessarily consciously) to favor her hypothesis. Other criticisms were more measured. "There's variability within individuals, and she shows that beautifully, but that doesn't mean there are no regions of the brain that, on average, are going to be different in men versus women," says neuroscientist Margaret M McCarthy of the University of Maryland School of Medicine, who studies sex differences in rats.

Joel, for her part, agrees that genetics, hormones and environment do create sex differences in the brain. She even agrees that given enough information about specific features in any one brain, it is possible to guess, with a high degree of accuracy, whether that brain belongs to a female or a male. But what you cannot do, she points out, is the reverse: look at any one man or woman and predict the topography and molecular landscape of that individual's brain or personality just because you know the person's sex.

Controversial as her study is, the essence of what Joel is saying is true, says Catherine Dulac, a molecular biologist at Harvard University whose work in mice echoes Joel's findings: "There is huge heterogeneity between individuals." Acknowledging that fact has opened a new thread in the conversation about what it means to be male or female. For neuroscientists, it is no longer enough to ferret out sex differences in the brain. The debate now centers on the source, size and significance of those differences. It could have major implications for how sex and gender are considered inside and outside the laboratory–and it may have consequences as well for whether drug regimens and treatment protocols should be specialized for women and men. "Our entire society is built on the assumption that our genitals divide us into two groups not just in terms of reproduction ability or possibility but also in terms of our brain or behavioral or psychological characteristics," Joel says. "People assume the differences add up. That if you are feminine in one characteristic, you will be feminine in other characteristics. But it's not true. Most humans have a gender mosaic."

Claims and Counterclaims

In the late 1800s, long before MRI was a gleam in any scientist's eye, the primary measurable difference in male and female brains was their weight (assessed postmortem, naturally). Because women's brains were, on average, five ounces lighter than men's, scientists declared that women must be less intelligent. As journalist Angela Saini recounts in *Inferior: How Science Got Women Wrong–and the New Research That's Rewriting the Story*, women's-rights advocate Helen Hamilton Gardener (a pseudonym) took on the experts of the day, arguing that the ratio of brain weight to body weight, or brain size to body size, had to be more relevant to intelligence than brain weight alone or "an elephant might out-think any of us." Fittingly, Gardener left her own brain to science. It was found to be five ounces lighter than the average male brain, but it was the same weight as that of the eminent male scientist who had founded the brain collection at Cornell University where her brain was stored. (For the record, Gardener was on to something. "Once you correct for brain size, most of these sex differences disappear, or they become very small," says Lise Eliot, a neuroscientist at the Chicago Medical School at Rosalind Franklin University of Medicine and Science.)

For much of the next century concrete sex differences in the brain were the province not of neuroscientists but endocrinologists, who studied sex hormones and mating behavior. Sex determination is a complex process that begins when a combination of genes on the X and Y chromosomes act in utero, flipping the switch on feminization or masculinization. But beyond reproduction and distinguishing boy versus girl, reports persisted of psychological and cognitive sex differences. Between the 1960s and early 1980s the late Stanford University psychologist Eleanor Maccoby found fewer differences than assumed: girls had stronger verbal abilities than boys, whereas boys did better on spatial and mathematical tests. Predictably, critiques followed. Janet Hyde, a psychologist at the University of Wisconsin–Madison, has conducted meta-analyses, combining the results of previous studies, and found, as she wrote in a 2016 study, that females perform as well as males in math and that "males and females are quite similar on most—but not all—psychological variables." Based on these results, Hyde developed what she calls the gender similarities hypothesis, which posits that the psychological makeup of men and women is more alike than different.

Once technology made it possible to peer inside a living brain, a long list of sex differences appeared that had nothing to do with mating or parenting. Writing in 2006 in *Nature Reviews Neuroscience*, Cahill described "a surge of findings from animals and humans concerning sex influences on many areas of brain and behaviour, including emotion, memory, vision, hearing, processing faces, pain perception, navigation, neurotransmitter levels, stress hormone action on the brain and disease states." In rats, McCarthy measures everything from the size of the collections of neurons that make up cell nuclei to the number of astrocytes and microglia, cells that form a support system for neurons. "There's irrefutable evidence of a biological basis for sex differences in the brain beginning from animals all the way up to humans," she says. But McCarthy also emphasizes that the source of sex differences in humans is more complicated than in animals that do not contend with gender, the psychological and social attributes of sex. "In humans, the fact that you're raised as a particular gender from the instant that you're born of itself exerts a biological impact on your brain," she says. In her 2009 book *Pink Brain, Blue Brain*, Eliot agrees, arguing that plasticity, the way the brain changes in response to experience, drives sex differences in behavior more than hardwired biology does.

Making the leap from brain to behavior provokes the most strident disagreements. One recent high-profile study accused of playing to stereotypes (and labeled "neurosexist") was a 2014 paper by Ruben Gur, Raquel Gur and Ragini Verma, all at the University of Pennsylvania. The group used diffusion tensor imaging, a technique showing the strength of connections among neurons, to look at nearly 1,000 brains of subjects between the ages of eight and 22. It found that males had stronger connections within the left and right hemispheres of the brain and that females had more robust links between hemispheres. The researchers concluded that "the results suggest that male brains are structured to facilitate connectivity between perception and coordinated action, whereas female brains are designed to facilitate communication between analytical and intuitive processing modes." (Counterclaim: the study did not correct for brain size.)

In Search of Variability

Into this maelstrom stepped Joel. Many previous studies have identified differences in single brain features and then used those differences to make claims about entire populations–the averages for women and men. Joel and her colleagues did the opposite: they used a picture of the population-level differences encountered across an entire group to ask what claims can be made about individual brains. "These are two different descriptions of the world," Joel says. Both show the same group-level differences. The critical question is: Which better describes human brains—the first, in which one type of brain is typical of males and another of females, or the second, in which most people's brains are mosaics of male and female characteristics?

Specifically, Joel's 2015 study asked two questions: How much overlap is there in features that show differences between females and males? And are brains "internally consistent"? The latter is a measure Joel developed to determine if all features in any one brain were masculine or feminine. Using four large sets of MRI data, her team identified, in each data set, several features with the greatest difference between males and females, such as the collective volume of the nerve cells' central bodies and dendritic extensions (gray matter) and their connecting fibers (white matter). They found a continuum of features. Definitive feminized and masculinized features occupied the extremes, and an intermediate zone exhibited a mix of attributes.

The researchers then assessed every brain in the data sets region by region and coded each feature. They reasoned that if brains are internally consistent, elements that show sex differences should reliably take on male or female forms. It followed that few brains should exist with both feminine and masculine traits. But between 23 to 53 percent of brains (depending on the data set) contained features from both ends of the spectrum. Brains that were internally consistent were rare—from 0 to 8 percent of those examined.

Joel cites arguments for the desirability of single-sex classrooms as a real-world example of why variability matters. "[Single-sex education] assumes that boys have one set of characteristics—for example, they are more active and have less patience—and girls have another set of characteristics. Therefore, we should separate them and treat each group differently. What we are showing is that although this is true at the group level, it's not true at the individual level. You can't divide students into a group that is very active, likes sports, is very good at mathematics, and doesn't like poetry and another group that is the mirror image. There are very few kids like this."

Most scientists find Joel's work demonstrating variability convincing. "Daphna's contribution was to show, individual by individual, the variability within gender," Eliot says. "Nobody ever publishes [those] data." But many find the measurement of internal consistency problematic. One response to Joel's *PNAS* paper was from Marco Del Giudice of the University of New Mexico and his colleagues. They argued that the definition Joel and her colleagues used for internal consistency was so extreme as to be biologically implausible, if not impossible. To prove it, they reran Joel's analysis using entirely different sets of biological variables—for example, comparing variability among facial features of three very different-looking monkey species. If Joel's method were valid, Del Giudice reasoned, the monkeys should show clear ("internally consistent") facial distinctions across species.

Despite notably varied appearances among the three species, the distinguishing facial features of any one monkey rarely resulted in internal consistency, as defined by Joel—hence, Cahill's view that the study is "rigged." In response, Joel and her colleagues used different analytical techniques in a 2018 study. Measuring similarity and difference mathematically rather than biologically in 2,176 human brains, they found that brains from females were almost as likely to be classified as "male" as brains from males are and that a male and a female are almost as likely to have the same brain types as two females or two males are.

The debate comes down to which matters more: the average or the individuals within the population under study. The answer often depends on the question being asked. But researchers can and do look at the same evidence and draw different conclusions. "The human brain may be a mosaic, but it is one with predictable patterns," wrote Avram Holmes of Yale University and his colleagues in response to Joel in 2015, and they believe those patterns demand statistical consideration. Biologist Anne Fausto-Sterling, a professor emerita of biology and gender development at Brown University and a critic of sex-difference research, has another perspective. "Talking about average differences is misleading if that's all we do," she says. "The brain is not a uniform entity that behaves as something male or something female, and it doesn't behave the same way in all contexts. Daphna is trying to get at the complexities of what brains actually do and how they function."

The implications of this controversy for science, especially clinical research aimed at treating disease, are considerable. Between 1997 and 2000, 10 drugs were withdrawn from the U.S. market because they carried side effects that were dangerous, even fatal. Eight of the 10 had greater health risks for women than for men. In 2013 the U.S. Food and Drug Administration reduced by half the prescription dosage of zolpidem, the generic name for Ambien, for women. After registering patients' complaints about drowsy morning commutes, researchers had discovered that the drug was still present in some women's bodies on waking. Here, too, counterclaims appear. Eliot and Sarah Richardson, a historian of science and gender at Harvard, suggest that much of the differences in zolpidem's side effects could be accounted for by body weight disparities. Weight is not the whole story, because women's higher body fat levels cause some drugs to metabolize more slowly, but precision in identifying the truly critical variables for drug dosing should be possible.

Partly in response to such concerns, starting in January 2016, the National Institutes of Health required that all preclinical research, the phase before testing in humans, must include female animals. Janine Clayton, director of the NIH Office of Research on Women's Health, was careful to say, in explaining the new policy, that including both sexes in studies does not necessarily mean looking for sex differences. Many regard this directive as an important step. McCarthy points out that various neurological diseases or disorders with an early onset, such as attention deficit hyperactivity disorder and autism spectrum disorder, are more common in males, whereas those that appear later, such as depression and anxiety, are more common in females. "In the face of that, we are compelled to look at the brain as a biological organ that differs in males and females," she says. "To not do it would be a travesty." But Joel, Fausto-Sterling and others worry that the pendulum will swing too far. They argue for research that includes sex as a variable, with an even number of male and female subjects, but that recognizes in analyzing results that "male" and "female" categories may reflect variables that have nothing to do with sex.

More broadly, if this work is to change the way society thinks about sex and gender, it might begin with terminology. "It's time to dump the word 'dimorphism,'" Eliot says. "A dimorphic structure is an ovary versus a testis. A 2 percent difference in gray matter to white matter ratio is not dimorphic. It's just a sex-related variance."

Dulac argues that we need "a more refined way to define these differences." In mice, she has found that neural circuits governing male mating behavior are also found in females, whereas maternal behavior circuits can be found in males. "It would be wrong to conclude from our work that there are no differences between males and females," Dulac says. "But the very interesting question is: How are these differences emerging, and how subtle or significant are they?"

McCarthy and Joel joined forces in 2017 to lay out a more sophisticated framework for defining what is being measured in sex-difference research and what it means. They suggest four possible dimensions: whether a trait is persistent or transient; whether it depends on context; whether it takes only one of two forms–and is thus truly dimorphic–or else falls on a spectrum; and whether it is a direct or indirect consequence of sex. This way of describing the world of sex differences is not nearly as catchy as the long-standing Mars versus Venus metaphor, but it is probably much more accurate. As a rule, complexity more closely reflects who people really are. "My mother is very nurturing, but she's a lot better at spatial navigation than my father," Eliot says. "That's a mosaic, right?

Referenced

Sex beyond the Genitalia: The Human Brain Mosaic. Daphna Joel et al. in *Proceedings of the National Academy of Sciences USA*, Vol. 112, No. 50, pages 15,468–15,473; December 15, 2015.

Incorporating Sex as a Biological Variable in *Neuropsychiatric Research: Where Are We Now and Where Should We Be?* Daphna Joel and Margaret M. McCarthy in *Neuropsychopharmacology*, Vol. 42, No. 2, pages 379–385; January 2017.

About the Author

Lydia Denworth is a Brooklyn, N.Y.–based science writer and a contributing editor for Scientific American. *She wrote about the neuroscience of stuttering in our August 2021 issue. She is co-author of* Parent Nation.

Promiscuous Men, Chaste Women and Other Gender Myths

By Cordelia Fine, Mark A. Elgar

One of Australia's more provocative art museums, the Museum of Old and New Art in Hobart, Tasmania, hosted in 2016 and 2017 an exhibition on the evolution of art. Three evolutionary scientists who guest-curated the show offered their perspectives on how evolution explains not just the characteristics of amoebas, ants and antelopes but also the uniquely human endeavor of art. One of these explanations sees art as an evolved trait akin to the peacock's effervescently colored tail, which increases its bearer's reproductive success by signaling superiority as a mate.

Hands up if this scenario conjures in your mind the image of a much feted female artist, famous for fearlessly pushing the boundaries of artistic convention, pleasurably making her way through a series of handsome young male muses? We didn't think so.

The stereotype of the daring, promiscuous male—and his counterpart, the cautious, chaste female—is deeply entrenched. Received wisdom holds that behavioral differences between men and women are hardwired, honed by natural selection over millennia to maximize their differing reproductive potentials. In this view, men, by virtue of their innate tendencies toward risk-taking and competitiveness, are destined to dominate at the highest level of every realm of human endeavor, whether it is art, politics or science.

But a closer look at the biology and behavior of humans and other creatures shows that many of the starting assumptions that have gone into this account of sex differences are wrong. For example, in many species, females benefit from being competitive or playing the field. And women and men often have similar preferences where their sex lives are concerned. It is also becoming increasingly clear that inherited environmental factors play a role in the development of adaptive behaviors; in humans, these factors include our gendered culture. All of which means that equality between the sexes might be more attainable than previously supposed.

Fast Males, Finicky Females

The origin of the evolutionary explanation of past and present gender inequality is Charles Darwin's theory of sexual selection. His observations as a naturalist led him to conclude that, with some exceptions, in the arena of courtship and mating, the challenge to be chosen usually falls most strongly on males. Hence, males, rather than females, have evolved characteristics such as a large size or big antlers to help beat off the competition for territory, social status and mates. Likewise, it is usually the male of the species that has evolved purely aesthetic traits that appeal to females, such as stunning plumage, an elaborate courtship song or an exquisite odor.

It was, however, British biologist Angus Bateman who, in the middle of the 20th century, developed a compelling explanation of *why* being male tends to lead to sexual competition. The goal of Bateman's research was to test an important assumption from Darwin's theory. Like natural selection, sexual selection results in some individuals being more successful than others. Therefore, if sexual selection acts more strongly on males than females, then males should have a greater range of reproductive success, from dismal failures to big winners. Females, in contrast, should be much more similar in their reproductive success. This is why being the animal equivalent of a brilliant artist, as opposed to a mediocre one, is far more beneficial for males than for females.

Bateman used fruit flies to test this idea. Although the technology for paternity testing did not exist at the time, he inferred parentage and the number of different mates of males and females as best he could. He did this rather ingeniously, by using fruit flies with different genetic mutations, including one that makes the bristles on the wings extra long, another that makes the wings curl upward, and yet another that renders the eyes very small or absent. These mutations are sometimes evident in offspring, so Bateman could estimate how many offspring each adult produced by counting the number of different mutants among the surviving offspring. From his data, he concluded that males were indeed more variable than females in their reproductive success (measured as offspring). Bateman also reported that only male reproductive success increased with the number of mates. This result, he argued, is why males compete and females choose: a male's reproductive success is largely limited by the number of females he can inseminate, whereas a female reaches her plateau with a single mate that provides her with all the sperm she needs.

Scholars mostly ignored Bateman's study at first. But some two decades later evolutionary biologist Robert Trivers, then at Harvard University, catapulted it into scientific fame. He expressed Bateman's idea in terms of greater female investment in reproduction–the big, fat egg versus the small, skinny sperm–and pointed out that this initial asymmetry can go well beyond the gametes to encompass gestation, feeding (including via lactation, in the case of mammals) and protecting. Thus, just as a consumer takes far more care in the selection of a car than of a disposable, cheap trinket, Trivers suggests that the higher-investing sex–usually the female–will hold out for the best possible partner with whom to mate. And here is the kicker: the lower-investing sex–typically the male–will behave in ways that, ideally, distribute cheap, abundant seed as widely as possible.

The logic is so elegant and compelling it is hardly surprising that contemporary research has identified many species to which the so-called Bateman-Trivers principles seem to apply, including species in which, unusually, it is *males* that are the higher-investing sex. For example, in some species of katydids, also known as bush crickets, the male's investment in reproduction is greater than the female's, thanks to a nutrient-rich package he provides, along with sperm, during copulation. Females thus fight one another for access to males.

The Bateman-Trivers principles also seem to provide a plausible explanation of the gender dynamics of human societies. Women are commonly understood to have less interest in casual sex with multiple partners, for instance, and to be more caring and less competitive and risk-taking. Applying the Bateman-Trivers logic, these behaviors serve to protect their investment. Contemporary advice from Facebook's chief operating officer Sheryl Sandberg to women to "lean in" at work to rise to the top thus appears to be undercut by arguments that predispositions to take risks and compete have evolved more strongly in males than in females because of greater reproductive return.

Breaking the Rules

But it turns out that nature is not nearly so simple and neat as this line of reasoning would suggest, even for nonhuman animals. In the decades since the Bateman-Trivers principles were forged, many of their foundational assumptions have been overturned. One such change in thinking concerns the supposed cheapness of reproduction for males. Sperm is not always cheap, nor is it always abundant: for instance, male stick insects can take several weeks to recover their libido after a lengthy copulation. And more recent scrutiny of the fruit fly's reproductive habits found that males do not always take up mating opportunities. Male selectivity has consequences for females of many insects, because if they mate with a male that has copulated extensively, they risk acquiring insufficient sperm. Scarce or limited sperm is not an uncommon challenge for females, which may mate repeatedly with different males precisely to acquire enough sperm.

In fact, a reexamination of Bateman's data from the lab of Patricia Gowaty of the University of California, Los Angeles, revealed, crucially, that a female fruit fly's reproductive success also increased with her mating frequency, a pattern that has emerged for a great many other species of animals. Furthermore, field studies show that mating for females is not the given scientists once assumed it to be. In a surprisingly large number of species, a significant proportion of females do not encounter a male and are thus unable to reproduce.

Nor is promiscuous mating standard practice for males. Monogyny, in which males mate only once, is not uncommon and can be an effective means of maximizing reproductive success.

Insects are not the only creatures that challenge the Bateman-Trivers principles. Even in mammals, for which investment in reproduction is particularly skewed because of the costs of gestation and lactation for females, competition is important not just for male reproductive success but also for female reproductive success. For example, the infants of higher-ranking female chimpanzees have higher rates of both arrival and survival than those of lower-ranking females.

In our own species, the traditional story is additionally complicated by the inefficiency of human sexual activity. Unlike many other species, in which coitus is hormonally coordinated to a greater or lesser degree to ensure that sex results in conception, humans engage in a vast amount of nonreproductive sex. This pattern has important implications. First, it means that any one act of coitus has a low probability of giving rise to a baby, a fact that should temper overoptimistic assumptions about the likely reproductive return on seed spreading. Second, it suggests that sex serves purposes beyond reproduction–strengthening relationships, for example.

Cultural and societal changes further necessitate rethinking the application of Bateman-Trivers principles to humans. The dichotomous view of the sexes that held sway in the last century has given way to one that sees differences mainly in degree rather than kind. Increased female sexual autonomy wrought by the birth-control pill and the sexual revolution has led to marked increases in premarital sex and numbers of sexual partners in women especially. And women and men report largely similar preferences for their sex lives. For example, the second British National Survey of Sexual Attitudes and Lifestyles, based on a random sample of more than 12,000 people between the ages of 16 and 44 surveyed around the turn of this century, found that 80 percent of men and 89 percent of women preferred monogamy.

Meanwhile the feminist movement increased women's opportunities to enter, and excel in, traditionally masculine domains. In 1920 there were just 84 women studying at the top 12 law schools that admitted women, and those female lawyers found it nearly impossible to find employment. In the 21st century women and men are graduating from law school in roughly equal numbers, and women made up about 18 percent of equity partners in 2015.

Risks and Benefits

As we zoom in from this broad-brush perspective on gender patterns to a fine-grained examination of sex differences in behavior, the familiar evolutionary story becomes even muddier. Consider risk-taking, once assumed to be a masculine personality trait, thanks to its role in enhancing male reproductive success. It turns out that people are quite idiosyncratic in the kinds of risks they are willing to take. The skydiver is no more likely to gamble money than the person who prefers to exercise in the safety of the gym. It is people's perception of the potential costs and benefits of a particular risky action, not their attitude toward risk per se, that explains their willingness to take risks. These perceived costs and benefits can include not only material losses and gains but also less tangible impacts on reputation or self-concept.

This nuance is important because sometimes the balance of risks and benefits is not the same for men and women because of physical differences between the sexes or gendered norms, or both. Consider, for example, the risk of a casual sexual encounter. For a man, the gains include the near certainty of an orgasm and perhaps a burnishing of his reputation as a "stud." For a woman, sexual pleasure is far less likely from casual sex, according to a large-scale study of North American students published in 2012 by Elizabeth Armstrong of the University of Michigan and her colleagues. And thanks to the sexual double standard, her reputation is more likely to be damaged by the episode. Among young Australians, for example, sociologist Michael Flood, now at the Queensland University of

Technology, found that the label "slut" retains a stronger "moral and disciplinary weight ... when applied to women." Moreover, a woman bears greater physical risks, including pregnancy, sexually transmitted disease and even sexual assault.

The lens of different risks and benefits can also clarify the sexes' different propensity to assert themselves at work, as Sandberg has advised women to do. It is hard to see how a young female lawyer, looking first at the many young women at her level and then at the very few female partners and judges, can be as optimistic about the likely payoff of leaning in and making sacrifices for her career as a young male lawyer. And this is before one considers the big-picture evidence of sexism, sexual harassment and sex discrimination in traditionally masculine professions such as law and medicine.

Still, the idea that a nonsexist society could erase the psychological effects of timeless, enduring sex differences in reproductive investment seems implausible to many. An article from 2017 in the *Economist*, for example, equated the marketing-inspired tradition of the diamond engagement ring with the strutting peacock's extravagant tail, an evolved courtship ritual that signals a man's resources and commitment. The journalist wrote that "greater equality for women might seem to render male-courtship displays redundant. But mating preferences evolved over millennia and will not change quickly."

Environmental Influence

Although sex certainly influences the brain, this argument overlooks the growing recognition in evolutionary biology that offspring do not just inherit genes. They also inherit a particular social and ecological environment that can play a critical role in the expression of adaptive traits. For example, adult male moths that hailed, as larvae, from a dense population develop particularly large testes. These enhanced organs stand the moths in good stead for engaging in intense copulatory competition against the many other males in the population. One would be forgiven for assuming that these generously sized gonads are a genetically determined adaptive trait. Yet adult male moths of the same species raised as larvae in a lower-density population instead develop larger wings and antennae, which are ideal for searching for widely dispersed females.

If the development of sex-linked physical characteristics can be influenced by the social environment, it stands to reason that sex-linked behavior can be, too. One striking example comes from the previously mentioned female katydids, which compete for the males that bring them both sperm and food, in line with the Bateman-Trivers principles. Remarkably, when their environment becomes rich with nutritious pollen, their competitive "nature" wanes.

The environment is similarly important for adaptive behavior in mammals. Research published starting in the late 1970s found that rat mothers care for male and female pups differently. The males get licked more than the females in the anogenital region because the mothers are attracted to the higher level of testosterone in male pups' urine. Intriguingly, the greater stimulation from this higher-intensity licking plays a part in the development of sex differences in parts of the brain involved in basic masculine mating behavior.

As University of Sydney philosopher of science Paul Griffiths has observed, we should not be surprised that environmental factors or experiences that reliably recur every generation should be incorporated as inputs into the developmental processes that bring about evolved traits.

In our own species, these developmental inputs include the rich cultural inheritance bestowed on every human newborn. And although social constructions of gender vary across time and place, all societies weight biological sex with heavy cultural meaning. Gender socialization starts at birth, and it would only make sense if the ruthless process of natural selection were to exploit it. It may well have been adaptive in our evolutionary past for males to take these and those risks or for females to avoid them. But when culture changes—creating a very different pattern of rewards, punishments, norms and consequences, compared with those in the past—so, too, will patterns of sex differences in behavior.

Thus, the *Economist* writer was not quite right in stating that human "mating preferences evolved over millennia and will not change quickly." True, they are unlikely to change as quickly as those of katydids, with a sprinkling of pollen (although we suspect that is not what was meant). There is usually nothing simple and quick about creating cultural shifts. But change certainly can, and certainly has, taken place over timescales shorter than millennia.

Take, for example, gender gaps in the importance men and women place on a partner's financial resources, attractiveness and chastity. The very quaintness of the term "chastity" to Western ears today compared with several decades ago speaks to rapid changes in cultural gender expectations. Cross-culturally, women and men from countries with greater gender equity are more similar in all these dimensions of partner preferences than those from countries with lower equity between the sexes, according to a 2012 study by Marcel Zentner and Klaudia Mitura, both then at the University of York in England. Research has also shown that in the U.S., men now place more importance on a female partner's financial prospects, education and intelligence—and care less about her culinary and housekeeping skills—than they did several decades ago. Meanwhile the cliché of the pitiable bluestocking spinster is a historical relic: although wealthier and better-educated women were once less likely to marry, now they are more likely to do so.

Could we, then, see the day when the world's finest art galleries display as much art by women as by men? We certainly shouldn't let Bateman's fruit flies tell us no.

Referenced

Sexual Selections: What We Can and Can't Learn about Sex from Animals. Marlene Zuk. University of California Press, 2002.

Rethinking Bateman's Principles: Challenging Persistent Myths of Sexually Reluctant Females and Promiscuous Males. Zuleyma Tang-Martínez in *Journal of Sex Research*, Vol. 53, Nos. 4–5, pages 532–559; 2016.

Inferior: How Science Got Women Wrong—And the New Research That's Rewriting the Story. Angela Saini. Beacon Press, 2017.

Testosterone Rex: Myths of Sex, Science, and Society. Cordelia Fine. W. W. Norton, 2017.

About the Authors

Cordelia Fine is a professor of history and philosophy of science at the University of Melbourne. Her most recent book, Testosterone Rex: Myths of Sex, Science, and Society *(W. W. Norton, 2017), won the 2017 Royal Society Insight Investment Science Book Prize.*

Mark A. Elgar is a professor of evolutionary biology at the University of Melbourne. His research group focuses on questions about the evolutionary significance of cooperative and mating behaviors and studies the role of chemical and visual communication in facilitating those behaviors.

When Sex and Gender Collide

By Kristina R. Olson

On arrival at a friend's house for dinner one night in the fall of 2008, I joined the evening's youngest guest, five-year-old Noah, who was playing on the couch. Little did I know he would single-handedly change the course of my career.

As a professor of developmental psychology, hanging out at the kids' table is not unusual for me. I study how children think about themselves and the people around them, and some of my keenest insights have come from conversations like this one. After some small talk, I saw Noah glance around the room, appear to notice that no one was looking and retrieve something from inside his pocket. The reveal was slow but the result unmistakable: a beloved set of Polly Pocket dolls.

Over the next few years I got to know Noah well and learned more about his past (all names of children here are pseudonyms to protect their privacy). Noah's parents had first noticed that he was different from his brother in the preschool years. He preferred female playmates and toys more commonly associated with girls, but his parents were unfazed. As he got older, Noah grew out his previously short hair and replaced his fairly gender-neutral wardrobe with one that prominently featured Twinkle Toes—shoes that lit up in pink as he stepped. Unlike many similar kids, Noah's family, friends and school fully accepted him. They even encouraged him to meet other kids like himself, boys who flouted gender norms. Along with the other adults in Noah's life, I couldn't help but wonder: What did Noah's behavior mean? Was he gay? Could he just be a kid who paid less attention to gender norms than most? At the time I had no idea that these questions would soon guide my scientific research.

Life for Noah started to change when he hit third and fourth grade. Noah recently explained how at this time, it became increasingly apparent that although people accepted his preferences and befriended him nonetheless, the way he saw himself—as a girl—

was at odds with the way others saw him. When people used his name and male pronouns, he realized that they thought of him as a boy. Noah remembers that this awareness made him increasingly unhappy—a feeling that had been rare just a few years earlier. According to his mom, previously cheerful and high-spirited Noah became sad and melancholy. This is when his family, after consulting with local therapists, reached a big decision that had been in the making for years. Noah came out as transgender, and accordingly Noah's friends, family and school community were asked to use a new name, Sarah, and to refer to Sarah as a girl.

At this point I had been studying developmental psychology for a decade, mostly looking into how young children think about the social categories—race, gender, social class—around them. In my free time, I looked for research about kids such as Sarah. Not a single quantitative study had investigated young children who had "switched" gender. ("Sex" refers to the biological categories male and female, whereas "gender" references one's identification with the social and cultural attributes and categories traditionally attached to each sex.) At that time nearly all adults who were transgender had transitioned much later in life, and almost no one had supported their early gender nonconformity (their desire to express preferences or behaviors that defy societal expectations for their sex). I wondered what we could learn about gender from such young pioneers as Sarah. What was the impact of transitioning on children's mental health and identity? What would this decision mean for their future?

How We Learn Gender

When most people hear about trans children, they are surprised. How could a three-year-old have such a clear sense of gender identity? People frequently compare early-identifying trans children with those who go through phases of believing they are cats or dinosaurs or who have imaginary friends. They use this comparison as evidence that no young child *knows* his or her identity or what is real or not real. Yet decades of work on gender development suggests these are precisely the ages at which nearly all kids are coming to understand their own and others' gender identities.

In Western cultures (where most of this research has been done), within the first year of life infants begin to distinguish people by sex, seeing individuals as either male or female. By about 18 months toddlers begin to understand gendered words such as "girl" or "man" and associate those words with sex-matched faces. By 24 months children know of sex stereotypes (such as associating women with lipstick), and before their third birthday nearly all kids label themselves and others with gender labels that match their sex.

During the preschool years, large numbers of young people go through what gender researchers May Ling Halim of California State University, Long Beach, and Diane Ruble of New York University call the "pink frilly dress stage": most girls become obsessed with frilly princess dresses or similarly "gendered" clothing, whereas many boys prefer superhero gear or formal wear and actively avoid pink. Around this time children also often exhibit strong preferences for the company of same-sex friends, engage in activities stereotypically associated with their sex and show a developing understanding that their sex is an enduring quality–believing that girls develop into women and boys into men.

Through the elementary school years, most children continue to associate themselves strongly with their sex group when asked both directly and indirectly. One experiment involves asking young participants to sort photographs of children on a computer screen into "boys" and "girls" while categorizing a set of words as either "me" words (like "me" and "myself") or "not me" words (like "they" and "them"). Researchers measure how quickly kids can make these categorizations when "boys" and "me" share one response key and "girls" and "not me" share another, compared with how quickly they can make the opposite pairings ("girls" with "me" and "boys" with "not me"). Past studies have found that an overwhelming majority of girls are faster at pairing "girls" with "me" and boys are faster at pairing "boys" with "me." Although scientists debate which aspects of development are innate or culturally constructed, or a combination of both, and not every child goes through the same gender pathway, most–including those children raised in families who vary in their parenting style, political beliefs, and racial and ethnic group membership–show the pattern we have described. And most parents, teachers and other adults never give it a second thought–except when kids start asserting that their gender is not what others expect it to be.

Early Differences

When I began the TransYouth Project in 2013, I wanted to understand whether, when and why young people such as Sarah do and do not behave like their peers in terms of their early gender development. The TransYouth Project is an ongoing study of hundreds of transgender and gender-nonconforming children. We focus on kids in the U.S. and Canada who are three to 12 years old when they begin the study, and we plan to follow them for 20 years.

What has been most surprising to me about our findings so far are the myriad ways in which trans kids' early gender development is remarkably similar to that of their peers. That is, children like Sarah look like other girls at every age but nothing like boys on measures of gender identity and preferences. Similarly, transgender boys (children who identify as boys but at birth were considered to be girls) perform like other boys on our tests. For example, one common observation in the preschool years is a strong hypergendered appearance–girls who *love* princess dresses; boys who avoid pink like it's the plague. We find the same thing in our youngest transgender children. The degree of their preferences for stereotypical clothes, as well as their tendency to prefer to befriend those of their self-identified gender and the degree to which they see themselves as members of their gender group, is statistically indistinguishable from their peers' responses on the same measures throughout the childhood years.

Furthermore, when predicting their identities into the future, trans girls see themselves becoming women and trans boys feel that they will be men, just as other girls and boys do. Even when we present children with more indirect or implicit measures of gender identity—the measures that assess reaction times rather than children's more explicit words and actions—we have found that trans girls see themselves as girls and trans boys see themselves as boys, suggesting that these identities are held at lower levels of conscious awareness. All this research combines to show that transgender identities in even very young children are surprisingly solid and consistent across measures, contradicting popular beliefs that such feelings are fleeting or that children are simply pretending to be the opposite gender.

The Roots of Gender

But where does the feeling of gender come from in the first place? The science is still far from conclusive. Because of how early this sense of identity can emerge, researchers have been looking for genetic and neuroanatomical signs in transgender people. One approach scientists often use in studying genetics is to look at twins. A major difference between identical and fraternal twins is that the former share more of their genetic material than the latter. If researchers find more agreement in transgender identity among identical twins than in fraternal twins, they infer that genetics play some role. And in fact, this is exactly what early studies are finding (although identical twins may also share more aspects of their socialization and environment). For example, in one 2012 review of the literature, Gunter Heylens of Ghent University in Belgium and his colleagues looked at 44 sets of same-sex twins in which at least one twin identified as transgender. They found that in nine of the 23 identical twin pairs, both siblings were transgender, whereas in no case among the 21 same-sex fraternal twin pairs were both twins transgender, suggesting transgender identity has some genetic underpinning. Despite these results, however, which particular genetic variations are involved is an open question.

Similarly, although some neuroscience studies have shown that brain structures of trans people resemble those of individuals with the same gender identity, rather than people with the same sex at birth, these findings have often involved small samples and have not yet been replicated. Further complicating interpretation of neuroscience results is the fact that brains change in response to experience, so even when differences appear, scientists do not know whether structural or functional brain differences *cause* the experience of a particular gender identity or *reflect* the experience of gender identity. Muddying the already murky waters, neuroscientists continue to debate whether even among people who are not transgender, there are reliable sex (or gender) differences in brains [see "Is There a 'Female' Brain?"]. Thus, whereas the topic is an active line of work in many research laboratories around the world, definitive conclusions about genetic and neural correlates of gender identity remain elusive.

Perhaps the most critical questions about transgender children, however, are about their well-being. Transgender adults and teens who did not go through the early social transition of kids such as Sarah and who were often rejected by peers and even their own families tend to have highly elevated rates of anxiety and depression. Estimates suggest that more than 40 percent of these largely unsupported trans teens and adults will attempt suicide. Many families like Sarah's report that these heartbreaking statistics are why they supported their children's early transitions.

My colleagues and I are finding—both in reports from parents and from kids themselves—that trans youth who make the social transition at a young age are doing remarkably well. They have depression rates comparable to their peers and only slightly elevated rates of anxiety. They also show very strong self-esteem. Whether these indicators of mental health stay strong as our cohort of trans children moves into the teen years remains to be seen, and certainly our all-volunteer sample is unlikely to be fully representative of all trans children alive today. Yet paired with work suggesting that interventions in adolescence (that involve not only social transitions but also hormonal therapy) are associated with improved mental health, these findings suggest that the high rates of depression, anxiety and suicide seen in earlier studies are not inevitable. Instead, as the world becomes more educated about transgender people, as rejection and bullying decrease, and as these youth receive support and intervention at earlier ages, we are optimistic that mental health risks will decrease.

"Pink Boys" and Tomboys

The first question I typically get when talking about transgender kids is something like, "Are you saying tomboys are actually transgender?" or "I used to be a boy who loved princess dresses. Are you suggesting I was transgender?" Of course, not all children who defy sex stereotypes as Sarah did are transgender. In fact, I would venture to say that most of them are not.

One such kid is Charlie. On the surface Charlie seemed a lot like Sarah early in life. Both were assumed to be boys at birth, and both showed signs by the preschool years that they were different. As with Sarah, Charlie loved all things feminine. His mom recalls that by age two, Charlie loved pink sparkly clothing and would put a towel over his head pretending it was hair. Much like Sarah's family, Charlie's family introduced him to other boys who loved feminine stuff. And over the years some of these children, like Sarah, socially transitioned. But Charlie did not. I recently asked Charlie about his decision not to transition. He explained that his family (sometimes with the help of a therapist) spent a lot of time talking about social transitions and made it clear that they were onboard if that was what he wanted. Charlie said he considered this possibility in the back of his mind for several years but ultimately decided that although he unabashedly liked stereotypically "girl" things (in fact the very day I interviewed him, Charlie was wearing pink shorts, a purple T-shirt and a pink scarf to school) and even if he occasionally uses a girl's name at camp, at the end of the day Charlie feels that he is a boy. As his mom explained, Charlie said that what he really wanted was for the world to accept him as he is–to let him wear what he wanted to wear and do what he wanted to do. But he did not truly feel he was a girl.

My work with children such as Charlie is ongoing, but preliminary data from others suggest that distinctive developmental trajectories may differentiate Sarah and Charlie. For instance, the degree to which a child gravitates to toys and clothes associated with the opposite gender may distinguish kids who ultimately identify as transgender from those who do not—on average, children like Sarah show even more gender nonconformity than children like Charlie. Other studies have suggested that the way kids talk about their gender identity—feeling you are a girl versus feeling that you wish the world was okay with your being a feminine boy (what Charlie's mom calls a "pink boy")—predicts the different paths of children like Sarah versus Charlie.

Researchers are also increasingly recognizing and studying people with nonbinary identities. Put simply, these are individuals who do not feel as if they are boys or girls, men or women, nor do they feel fully masculine or feminine. Instead many nonbinary people fall somewhere in the middle of a spectrum from masculine to feminine. To date, our research team has worked with several children who see themselves this way, but this group is not yet large enough from which to draw any strong conclusions.

What is undoubtedly true is that scientists have much to learn about children such as Sarah and Charlie. What does it mean to have a sense of yourself as a boy or a girl or something else? What makes a child more or less likely to identify that way? And how can we help all kids to be comfortable with themselves? Finding answers is especially difficult because gender is defined by culture, which constantly changes. In 1948, for instance, only 32 percent of adults believed women should wear slacks in public. Certainly feminine boys and masculine girls are not new; they are widely recognized in many indigenous cultures.

Today 14-year-old Sarah and 13-year-old Charlie are self-confident, smart and hardworking teens. Sarah plays piano, varsity field hockey and recently took up track. Charlie plays in a band and performs in theater. Both kids are popular and spend more of their time worrying about doing well in school and the complexities of adolescent social networks than about their gender. Both look to the future, excited about the possibilities that await them in college and beyond. Sarah says she wants to raise children with her future husband and aspires to make the world better for trans young people like herself. Charlie has dreams of moving to New York City to perform on Broadway. Both teens hope one day kids like them will be accepted for who they are regardless of the gender labels they use. In that hope, surely all of us can agree.

Referenced

Mental Health and Self-Worth in Socially Transitioned Transgender Youth. Lily Durwood et al. in Journal of the *Academy of Child and Adolescent Psychology*, Vol. 56, No. 2, pages 116–123.e2; February 2017.

The TransYouth Project: http://depts.washington.edu/transyp

About the Author

Kristina R. Olson is a professor of psychology at Princeton University, where she directs the Human Diversity Lab and the TransYouth Project.

The Disturbing History of Research into Transgender Identity

By Jack Turban

In 1975 psychiatrist Robert Stoller of the University of California, Los Angeles, wrote something bizarre in his textbook on sex and gender. He asserted that people who were assumed to be boys when they were born but whose gender identity or expression did not match that assumption "often have pretty faces, with fine hair, lovely complexions, graceful movements, and—especially—big, piercing, liquid eyes." Based on this observation, he suggested a theoretical model in which transgender girls become transgender because they are especially cute. Society treats them more like girls, he reasoned, and because of this experience, they start to identify as female.

As a physician-scientist, I'm generally of the opinion that knowledge leads to progress. But studies focused on this particular question—those asking what determines someone's gender identity—have led us down some strange and dangerous paths. Researchers in this area appear to be in search of some objective truth, but the science is rooted in a subjective assumption: that we need to know what makes someone transgender so that they can be "fixed." As a result, scientists have relentlessly pursued such questions, launching studies that promoted ideas that could hurt transgender children and their families.

Stoller's observations motivated many of the psychological theories behind what makes people transgender. In 1993 a group of researchers at the Clarke Institute of Psychiatry in Toronto set out to test his hypothesis that beauty and what was then called "gender identity disorder" were linked. They recruited 17 birth-assigned boys with the diagnosis and 17 birth-assigned boys without it, all around the age of eight. The researchers then took headshots of the children and showed them to 36 college students. The students were asked to rate the youngsters' physical appearance on a scale from one to five with categories such as "attractive," "handsome" and "beautiful." In the end, the college students found the children with "gender identity disorder" to be "prettier" than the cisgender boys. The findings seem to suggest Stoller was right: perhaps, because of their appearance, people treated the youngsters in the former group more like girls, and consequently, they became transgender. Though as the authors mention later in the paper, an equally plausible theory is that these children could have altered their appearance (long hair, et cetera) in ways that matched their identity, leading the college students to associate them with more feminine descriptions such as "pretty."

A few years later, researchers revived this line of investigation, using the headshots of young birth-assigned girls with "gender identity disorder." A group of college students again rated how "ugly" or "pretty" these children appeared, compared with cisgender girls. The children with "gender identity disorder" were rated as less beautiful, prompting the researchers to suggest that they may have been treated more like boys and thus identified as male. It seems more likely that these children simply cut their hair shorter, so the participants attached more masculine words to them. In the end, the study didn't reveal much about what makes someone transgender, but it did promote an offensive theory with the potential to diminish the self-esteem of vulnerable transgender youth.

Researchers also studied the parents of such children. Psychiatry has long been enamored with the theory of mothers harming the development of their children (for example, the refrigerator mother theory posited that autism was caused by a lack of maternal warmth). These studies similarly asked if perhaps parents were to "blame" for their kids' gender identity. In one paper, researchers assessed whether the mothers of children with "gender identity disorder" had more symptoms of either depression or a condition called borderline personality disorder. They found these mothers had more symptoms of both. Sounds convincing, right? Children must become transgender because their mothers are mentally ill.

What the researchers failed to discuss was that the mothers' symptoms could easily have been caused by the way society treated their children. The subscale of borderline personality disorder that was higher among them was "interpersonal conflict." You don't need to be the parent of a transgender child to imagine that raising your kid in an unaccepting community could create substantial conflict.

In another study, researchers noted that parents of children with "gender identity disorder" did not place strong limits on stereotypically gender atypical behaviors such as birth-assigned boys playing with dolls or birth-assigned girls playing with blocks or transportation toys. Perhaps this was the cause of the "problem"? If these parents had simply cracked down on this behavior early on—ripped the Barbie out of their toddler's hands, say—they may have prevented it, the authors posited. The more likely explanation is that it's difficult to take a doll away from a child who desperately wants to play with it. And that doing so makes them sad and impacts their self-esteem.

In each case, researchers were hyperfocused on finding a problem with either the kids or their parents. But in the end, these scientists failed to establish one. They seemed less interested in a vital reframing: perhaps the issue was not the children's identity but the way society treated them. Instead of supporting these kids, the researchers labeled them unattractive or painted their parents as mentally unstable.

These theories on the origins of gender identity have only added to the misguided, and increasingly illegal, calls for "therapies" designed to make transgender people cisgender. The logic of so-called gender identity conversion therapy is that if the environment is the cause, then we can simply alter the environment to nip things in the bud. Most of the "conversion" manuals have not been released to the public, but in 2002 a psychologist at Columbia University published "Gender Identity Disorder in Young Boys: A Parent and Peer-Based Protocol," which included parenting techniques such as "letting go of [the] boy by [the] mother," forcing the child to play with same-sex friends, and removing the youngster from stereotypically gender-atypical activities such as gymnastics or ballet. Notably, a recent study my colleagues and I conducted showed that attempts to change a child's gender identity from transgender to cisgender are associated with greater odds of attempting suicide. Several U.S. states have banned conversion therapy, but in much of the U.S., these practices continue.

Similar research into the psychological causes of transgender identity continues even today. A physician at Brown University recently conducted an anonymous survey of respondents recruited via Web sites for parents who believe peer pressure and online influences have made their children transgender. The survey essentially asked the parents if they thought the Internet made their children trans, and the parents, not surprisingly, given that they were visiting websites about this idea, answered yes. Conservative media latched onto the study, suggesting that transgender children are really just confused kids tricked into being transgender after reading something on Reddit. The implication is that we need to take these kids away from supportive online LGBTQ communities so that they can be made cisgender again. Reading through this literature, we need to ask ourselves some questions: What is the reason for this research? What does it hope to accomplish? The tireless search reveals a thinly veiled dogma: that being transgender is a pathology to be fixed. This belief not only harms transgender people but also undermines good science.

What good science shows us is that when we accept transgender people, they thrive. Instead of trying to figure out what went "wrong," we should be investing our time and energy into advocating for nondiscrimination laws, increasing access to health care and raising transgender voices in the media, so society realizes that they are vital members of our communities. Maybe Stoller was right when he noted that those children were exceptional. It's time we celebrate that and move on.

About the Author

Jack Turban is a fellow in child and adolescent psychiatry at the Stanford University School of Medicine, where he researches the mental health of transgender youth. His writing has appeared in the New York Times, *the* Washington Post, *the* Los Angeles Times, *and more. Follow him on Twitter@ jack_turban.*

What the Science on Gender-Affirming Care for Transgender Kids Really Shows

By Heather Boerner

For the first 40 years of their life, Texas resident Kelly Fleming spent a portion of most years in a deep depression. As an adult, Fleming–who uses they/them pronouns and who asked to use a pseudonym to protect their safety–would shave their face in the shower with the lights off so neither they nor their wife would have to confront the reality of their body.

What Fleming was experiencing, although they did not know it at the time, was gender dysphoria: the acute and chronic distress of living in a body that does not reflect one's gender and the desire to have bodily characteristics of that gender. While in therapy, Fleming discovered research linking access to gender-affirming hormone therapy with reduced depression in transgender people. They started a very low dose of estradiol, and the depression episodes became shorter, less frequent and less intense. Now they look at their body with joy.

So when Fleming sees what authorities in Texas, Alabama, Florida and other states are doing to bar transgender teens and children from receiving gender-affirming medical care, it infuriates them. And they are worried for their children, ages 12 and 14, both of whom are agender–an identity on the transgender spectrum that is neither masculine nor feminine.

"I'm just so excited to see them being able to present themselves in a way that makes them happy," Fleming says. "They are living their best life regardless of what others think, and that's a privilege that I did not get to have as a younger person."

Laws Based on "Completely Wrong" Information

Currently more than a dozen state legislatures or administrations are considering–or have already passed–laws banning health care for transgender young people. On April 20 the Florida Department of Health issued guidance to withhold such gender-affirming care. This includes social gender transitioning–acknowledging that a young person is trans, using their correct pronouns and name, and supporting their desire to live publicly as the gender of their experience rather than their sex assigned at birth. This comes nearly two months after Texas Governor Greg Abbott issued an order for the Texas Department of Family and Protective Services to investigate for child abuse parents who allow their transgender preteens and teenagers to receive medical care. Alabama recently passed SB 184, which would make it a felony to provide gender-affirming medical care to transgender minors. In Alabama, a "minor" is defined as anyone 19 or younger.

If such laws go ahead, 58,200 teens in the U.S. could lose access to or never receive gender-affirming care, according to the Williams Institute at the University of California, Los Angeles. A decade of research shows such treatment reduces depression, suicidality and other devastating consequences of trans preteens and teens being forced to undergo puberty in the sex they were assigned at birth.

The bills are based on "information that's completely wrong," says Michelle Forcier, a pediatrician and professor of pediatrics at Brown University. Forcier literally helped write the book on how to provide evidence-based gender care to young people. She is also an assistant dean of admissions at the Warren Alpert Medical School of Brown University. Those laws "are absolutely, absolutely incorrect" about the science of gender-affirming care for young people, she says. "[Inaccurate information] is there to create drama. It's there to make people take a side."

The truth is that data from more than a dozen studies of more than 30,000 transgender and gender-diverse young people consistently show that access to gender-affirming care is associated with better mental health outcomes–and that lack of access to such care is associated with higher rates of suicidality, depression and self-harming behavior. (Gender diversity refers to the extent to which a person's gendered behaviors, appearance and identities are culturally incongruent with the sex they were assigned at birth. Gender-diverse people can identify along the transgender spectrum, but not all do.) Major medical organizations, including the American Academy of Pediatrics (AAP), the American Academy of Child and Adolescent Psychiatry, the Endocrine Society, the American Medical Association, the American Psychological Association and the American Psychiatric Association, have published policy statements and guidelines on how to provide age-appropriate gender-affirming care. All of those medical societies find such care to be evidence-based and medically necessary.

AAP and Endocrine Society guidelines call for developmentally appropriate care, and that means no puberty blockers or hormones until young people are already undergoing puberty for their sex assigned at birth. For one thing, "there are no hormonal differences among prepubertal children," says Joshua Safer, executive director of the Mount Sinai Center for Transgender Medicine and Surgery in New York City and co-author of the Endocrine Society's guidelines. Those guidelines provide the option of gonadotropin-releasing hormone analogues (GnRHas), which block the release of sex hormones, once young people are already into the second of five puberty stages—marked by breast budding and pubic hair. These are offered only if a teen is not ready to make decisions about puberty. Access to gender-affirming hormones and potential access to gender-affirming surgery is available at age 16—and then, in the case of transmasculine youth, only mastectomy, also known as top surgery. The Endocrine Society does not recommend genital surgery for minors.

Before puberty, gender-affirming care is about supporting the process of gender development rather than directing children through a specific course of gender transition or maintenance of cisgender presentation, says Jason Rafferty, co-author of AAP's policy statement on gender-affirming care and a pediatrician and psychiatrist at Hasbro Children's Hospital in Rhode Island. "The current research suggests that, rather than predicting or preventing who a child might become, it's better to value them for who they are now—even at a young age," Rafferty says.

A Safe Environment to Explore Gender

A 2021 systematic review of 44 peer-reviewed studies found that parent connectedness, measured by a six-question scale asking about such things as how safe young people feel confiding in their guardians or how cared for they feel in the family, is associated with greater resilience among teens and young adults who are transgender or gender-diverse. Rafferty says he sees his role with regard to prepubertal children as offering a safe environment for the child to explore their gender and for parents to ask questions. "The gender-affirming approach is not some railroad of people to hormones and surgery," Safer says. "It is talking and watching and being conservative."

Only once children are older, and if the incongruence between the sex assigned to them at birth and their experienced gender has persisted, does discussion of medical transition occur. First a gender therapist has to diagnose the young person with gender dysphoria.

After a gender dysphoria diagnosis—and only if earlier conversations suggest that hormones are indicated—guidelines call for discussion of fertility, puberty suppression and hormones. Puberty-suppressing medications have been used for decades for cisgender children who start puberty early, but they are not meant to be used indefinitely. The Endocrine Society guidelines recommend a maximum of two years on GnRHa therapy to allow more time for children to form their gender identity before undergoing puberty for their sex assigned at birth, the effects of which are irreversible.

"[Puberty blockers] are part of the process of 'do no harm,'" Forcier says, referencing a popular phrase that describes the Hippocratic Oath, which many physicians recite a version of before they begin to practice.

Hormone blocker treatment may have side effects. A 2015 longitudinal observational cohort study of 34 transgender young people found that, by the time the participants were 22 years old, trans women experienced a decrease in bone mineral density. A 2020 study of puberty suppression in gender-diverse and transgender young people found that those who started puberty blockers in early puberty had lower bone mineral density *before* the start of treatment than the public at large. This suggests, the authors wrote, that GnRHa use may not be the cause of low bone mineral density for these young people. Instead they found that lack of exercise was a primary factor in low bone-mineral density, especially among transgender girls.

Other side effects of GnRHa therapy include weight gain, hot flashes and mood swings. But studies have found that these side effects—and puberty delay itself—are reversible, Safer says.

Gender-affirming hormone therapy often involves taking an androgen blocker (a chemical that blocks the release of testosterone and other androgenic hormones) and estrogen in transfeminine teens, and testosterone supplementation in transmasculine teens. Such hormones may be associated with some physiological changes for adult transgender people. For instance, transfeminine people taking estrogen see their so-called "good" cholesterol increase. By contrast, transmasculine people taking testosterone see their good cholesterol decrease. Some studies have hinted at effects on bone mineral density, but these are complicated and also depend on personal, family history, exercise, and many other factors in addition to hormones."

And while some critics point to a decade-old study and older studies suggesting very few young people persist in transgender identity into late adolescence and adulthood, Forcier says the data are "misleading and not accurate." A recent review detailed methodological problems with some of these studies. New research in 17,151 people who had ever socially transitioned found that 86.9 percent persisted in their gender identity. Of the 2,242 people who reported that they reverted to living as the gender associated with the sex they were assigned at birth, just 15.9 percent said they did so because of internal factors such as questioning their experienced gender but also because of fear, mental health issues and suicide attempts. The rest reported the cause was social, economic and familial stigma and discrimination. A third reported that they ceased living openly as a trans person because doing so was "just too hard for me."

The Harms of Denying Care

Data suggest the effects of denying that care are worse than whatever side effects result from delaying sex-assigned-at-birth puberty. And medical society guidelines conclude that the benefits of gender-affirming care outweigh the risks. Without gender-affirming hormone therapy, cisgender hormones take over, forcing body changes that can be permanent and distressing.

A 2020 study of 300 gender-incongruent young people found that mental distress–including self-harm, suicidal thoughts and depression–increased as the children were made to proceed with puberty according to their assigned sex. By the time 184 older teens (with a median age of 16) reached the stage in which transgender boys began their periods and grew breasts and transgender girls' voice dropped and facial hair began to appear, 46 percent had been diagnosed with depression, 40 percent had self-harmed, 52 percent had considered suicide, and 17 percent had attempted it–rates significantly higher than those of gender-incongruent children who were a median of 13.9 years old or of cisgender kids their own age.

Conversely, access to gender-affirming hormones in adolescence appears to have a protective effect. In one study, researchers followed 104 teens and young adults for a year and asked them about their depression, anxiety and suicidality at the time they started receiving hormones or puberty blockers and again at the three-month, six-month and one-year mark. At the beginning of the study, which was published in *JAMA Network Open* in February 2022, more than half of the respondents reported moderate to severe depression, half reported moderate to severe anxiety, and 43.3 percent reported thoughts of self-harm or suicide in the past two weeks.

But when the researchers analyzed the results based on the kind of gender-affirming care the teens had received, they found that those who had access to puberty blockers or gender-affirming hormones were 60 percent less likely to experience moderate to severe depression. And those with access to the medical treatments were 73 percent less likely to contemplate self-harm or suicide.

"Delays in prescribing puberty blockers and hormones may in fact worsen mental health symptoms for trans youth," says Diana Tordoff, an epidemiology graduate student at the University of Washington and co-author of the study.

That effect may be lifelong. A 2022 study of more than 21,000 transgender adults showed that just 41 percent of adults who wanted hormone therapy received it, and just 2.3 percent had access to it in adolescence. When researchers looked at rates of suicidal thinking over the past year in these same adults, they found that access to hormone therapy in early adolescence was associated with a 60 percent reduction in suicidality in the past year and that access in late adolescence was associated with a 50 percent reduction.

For Fleming's kids in Texas, gender-affirming hormones are not currently part of the discussion; not all trans people desire hormones or surgery to feel affirmed in their gender. But Fleming is already looking at jobs in other states to protect their children's access to such care, should they change their mind. "Getting your body closer to the gender [you] identify with–that is what helps the dysphoria," Fleming says. "And not giving people the opportunity to do that, making it harder for them to do that, is what has made the suicide rate among transgender people so high. We just–trans people are just trying to survive."

If You Need Help

If you or someone you know is struggling or having thoughts of suicide, help is available. Call or text 988 to be connected to the National Suicide Prevention Lifeline. The Lifeline offers the free, confidential, 24/7 support of trained counselors to help those in emotional distress. An online 988 Lifeline chat is also available at 988lifeline.org. The three-digit number became available in July 2022 to replace the 1-800-273-8255 (TALK) number, but this original number still also connects callers to the Lifeline.

About the Author

Heather Boerner is a health care and science journalist based in Pittsburgh. Her work has appeared in the Daily Beast, *the* Washington Post, *the* Atlantic, *and NPR. Follow her on Twitter @HeatherBoerner.*

The Search for a 'Cause' of Transness Is Misguided

By Nat Mulkey

Scientists have been engaging for decades in an avid hunt for a biological explanation for why some people are transgender. This urge to find a biological explanation for the existence of trans, and, more generally, LGBTQ, folks was born out of the need to confront the harmful discourse trumpeted by some Christian Right organizations that being gay or transgender is a sinful choice people make. Taken to the extreme, this rhetoric is used to justify the existence and continued perpetuation of the so-called "cure" known as conversion therapy–a practice long considered harmful to LGBTQ individuals and denounced by multiple medical bodies. The search for a biological cause of transness–also known as "biological essentialism"–may be well-intentioned, but it is a dangerous path that leaves little room for a real understanding of gender and gender identity.

Most of the investigation into the biological basis of transness has been in the field of neuroscience. Postmortem studies conducted by Dick Swaab of the Netherlands Institute for Neuroscience suggested multiple differences in brain structure between transgender and cisgender individuals. These differences seem to indicate that transgender women and men have brain structures more similar to the brains of cisgender individuals of the same gender identity than cisgender individuals of the gender they were assigned at birth. More recently, the field has moved from postmortem brain analysis to functional MRI studies. Cisgender men and women have previously been shown to have different brain areas engaged during a spatial-reasoning task. This research team found that both cisgender boys and transgender boys (assigned female at birth and on pubertal suppression therapy) had similar activation patterns during the task, compared to cisgender girls.

While the hunt for a cause marches on, the darker potential of the biological essentialism argument is becoming more evident. Biological essentialism, or belief in the claim that there is a biological basis for being transgender, does not equate to acceptance of transgender individuals. In 2017 researchers Boby Ho-Hong Ching and Jason Teng Xu exposed a group of university students to three articles of varying support for the idea that gender differences have a biological basis and then evaluated the students' degree of transgender prejudice. Those exposed to the article with the most bioessentialist view demonstrated increased prejudice toward transgender individuals, compared with the other two groups. There has also been research showing that the isolated belief in the innateness of sexual orientation did not translate to positive attitudes toward sexual minority groups.

The other problem with the bioessentialist perspective is the support it lends to arguments that there is something broken or fixable about transgender individuals. One article published in 2018 in *Clinical Psychopharmacology and Neuroscience* claims that the brain structure differences found in transgender individuals arise from their chosen lifestyle and that "transgender individuals can be driven toward culturally contextualized behaviors ... and can be adapted to their original biological gender through trying to enjoy a natural sexual relationship." This is a clear example of the biological essentialist perspective being used to argue for and justify a "cure"–in this case, what sounds like the equivalent of conversion therapy.

Lastly, the continued push for the bioessentialist model wrongly and inevitably delegitimizes many transgender or nonbinary individuals' experiences. There is a privileged transgender narrative in society: one that fits the medical, historical and academic expectations of what transitioning entails. This acceptable transgender narrative includes a linear transition (from social to hormonal and finally to surgical) and a binary transition (from male to female or female to male). This narrative fails to capture the reality of transgender or nonbinary (TGNB) experiences, however.

The paths people take to their authentic gender identity are as numerous as any other component of an individual's story.

This view is more in line with a contemporary understanding of gender, not so much as something that is given to us, but as something dynamic and relational. Florence Ashley, a transfeminine jurist and bioethicist, wrote in *Clinical Child Psychology and Psychiatry* that "gender is not something given that we need to unearth, but something that remakes itself—the same or anew—over and over again as we gather new experiences of the world.... Transitioning is just another way we explore our gender." The bioessentialist model encourages a flawed dynamic with clinical or academic individuals as the assessors of accuracy and the TGNB individuals as the justify-or-die subject. As Ashley states, "we must move away from attempting to assess the truth and authenticity of assertions of gender identity."

An individual should not need to justify their gender identity any more than someone would need to justify their eye color. While intriguing and often well-intentioned, the continued search for a biological basis of transness needs to be reconsidered and possibly ended altogether. At the very least, proponents of this search need to supplement it with vocal and ardent messages that use of this research to assess someone's true "transness" is an error that robs them of their autonomy and authentic identity.

About the Author

Nat Mulkey is a transgender nonbinary writer and fourth-year medical student at Boston University School of Medicine (BUSM). They write both personal narratives and articles about ethics and contemporary LGBTQI+ issues in relation to health care, and also work on the LGBTQI+ curriculum at BUSM.

Section 3: Using Science to Explain Your Tastes and Beliefs

In Teen Music Choices, Anxiety Rules

By Abigail Baird

In 2009, Miley Cyrus reportedly made an astonishing 25 million dollars. Most of that money came from album sales, which were reported to be slightly over 4 million during that year. Four million... Four million?! Have you heard Miley Cyrus sing? Are there really four million kids out there willing to spend their hard-earned babysitting money on a Miley Cyrus album because they deeply love listening to her sing? Well, according to the findings of a study recently published in *Neuroimage*, selling four million albums does not translate to having four million people like your music. The study reports that there is good reason to believe that a lot of those purchases were made out of fear–a fear well known to adolescents all over America: terror of social rejection.

The fear of social rejection is so strong in adolescents because their relationships are essential for passing on the lessons that will enable them to join adult society. In order to do this properly and efficiently, teenagers come equipped with the ability to learn fast and furiously from their peers, especially those who wield more social power–who are older or more popular. Although this system developed because it helps the teen transition to adulthood, it has proven an excellent principle upon which to base economic decisions. The popular kids dictate teen culture, and if they endorse it (Twilight, anyone?) it will sell.

Gregory S. Berns, the chair of Neuroeconomics at Emory University, and his colleagues set out to understand more about the neural and behavioral mechanics of social influence on decisions about purchasing music. The researchers' basic question was: When people change their behavior based on social influence, is it their actual preferences that change, or simply their behavior? In order to investigate this question they designed a clever behavioral study that was amenable to being performed while participants had their brains scanned.

The researchers chose to study adolescents between the ages of 12 and 17, a cohort thought to be highly susceptible to social influence, and known to buy at least one third of albums in the United States. Each participant heard a short clip of a song downloaded from the social-networking website Myspace. Following the clip they were asked to make two ratings, one indicating how familiar they were with the clip (which was always the hook or chorus of the chosen song) and one indicating how much they liked the clip on a five point scale. The clip was then played a second time, and they were again asked to rate how much they liked the song. However, in two thirds of these second trials the teens were shown a popularity rating that was estimated based on the number of times the song was downloaded.

When no information about the popularity of a song was displayed, teens changed their likability rating of the song 12 percent of the time. Not surprisingly, after being shown the popularity of a song, teens changed their ratings more frequently, on average 22 percent of the time. This difference was highly significant, and it is worth noting that among those who changed their likability ratings, 79 percent of the time teens changed their ratings in the direction of the popularity rating–they followed the crowd.

These behavioral findings validate a great deal of previous research on conformity, and demonstrate that it is alive and well in the average American adolescent. Although these results are compelling, they do not address whether or not teens were actually "following the crowd" or, upon further reflection and information from their peers, changed their intrinsic preference for a particular piece of music. To investigate this question, Berns and his colleagues looked to brain activity.

Their logic was simple: Using the first rating of the songs, it would be possible to find a network of brain regions that related to individuals' reports of liking the music. If, after they changed their minds in the second rating, this network appeared again, then it would suggest that the adolescents really did change how much they liked the music based on the influence of their peers.

If, on the other hand, a different network of regions revealed itself following a change in likability rating, this would be more in line with the notion that teens were simply complying with their peers.

Liking of songs, based on teens' initial ratings was strongly related to activity in the head of the caudate nucleus. Although the exact nature of caudate activity remains a source of debate, most agree that activity in this area is highly related to reward and valuation. So it appears to reflect pleasure, not familiarity. The researchers also observed activity in a number of regions that have been previously associated with the pleasurable aspects of listening to music.

When adolescents changed their ratings, according to their brain activity, it had nothing to do with increased liking of the music. Instead, a very different picture emerged. The network of regions associated with changing a rating included bilateral insula, the anterior cingulate cortex and the supplementary motor cortex and frontal poles–regions previously associated with anxiety and pain. These regions all showed increased activity when teens were shown a popularity rating that did not match their own, meaning that they had this neural response prior to changing their own rating. Interestingly, individuals who demonstrated the greatest sensitivity to popularity, as determined by survey measures taken at the beginning of the study, manifested the strongest insula activity during the act of conforming. Simply, the greater the insula activity, the higher the odds of conforming. The authors suggest that this pattern of activity can be explained by cognitive or emotional dissonance caused by the mismatch between one's ratings and the ratings of others.

So, the authors argue, conforming seems to be motivated not by the positive utility of behaving like your peers, but instead out of anxiety and pain at the prospect of being a "contrarian." Again, this points to the function of peer influence during adolescence. During adolescence, peers wield considerable coercive power–that is, friends are quick to dispense disapproval, teasing and rejection when social norms are not followed. The pain of being rejected by one's peer group can be a matter of life or death, as recent cyber-bullying cases in the news demonstrate.

So what does this study mean practically? Well, there are very different implications for commerce and parents. In terms of marketing, if you want to sell a lot of albums, get the popular kids hooked, and their endorsement will cause enough fear among their overly attentive peers to make the music sell. The idea of being able to relate to another teen for only $12.95 is very appealing to adolescents, who are consumed with trying to maintain their status in their peer groups.

For parents the implications are a little different. Take heart from these findings. It is likely the case that your teenagers do not actually like the terrible music you hear during those brief moments when they take their ear buds out. In fact, the researchers found that adolescents who were most sensitive to the ratings of others engaged in much less active listening (which is particularly encouraging given the lyrics of some popular music). The bottom line for parents is that if your adolescents' need for the latest Hannah Montana album keeps them in step with their peer group, take it as a sign that they are aware of their culture–and this type of conformity is often predictive of a teen eventually becoming a well-adjusted adult.

About the Author

Abigail Baird is an assistant professor of psychology at Vassar College who studies brain development in adolescence.

Conservative and Liberal Brains Might Have Some Real Differences

By Lydia Denworth

In 1968 a debate was held between conservative thinker William F. Buckley, Jr., and liberal writer Gore Vidal. It was hoped that these two members of opposing intellectual elites would show Americans living through tumultuous times that political disagreements could be civilized. That idea did not last for long. Instead Buckley and Vidal descended rapidly into name-calling. Afterward, they sued each other for defamation.

The story of the 1968 debate opens a well-regarded 2013 book called *Predisposed*, which introduced the general public to the field of political neuroscience. The authors, a trio of political scientists at the University of Nebraska-Lincoln and Rice University, argued that if the differences between liberals and conservatives seem profound and even unbridgeable, it is because they are rooted in personality characteristics and biological predispositions.

On the whole, the research shows, conservatives desire security, predictability and authority more than liberals do, and liberals are more comfortable with novelty, nuance and complexity. If you had put Buckley and Vidal in a magnetic resonance imaging machine and presented them with identical images, you would likely have seen differences in their brain, especially in the areas that process social and emotional information. The volume of gray matter, or neural cell bodies, making up the anterior cingulate cortex, an area that helps detect errors and resolve conflicts, tends to be larger in liberals. And the amygdala, which is important for regulating emotions and evaluating threats, is larger in conservatives.

While these findings are remarkably consistent, they are probabilities, not certainties—meaning there is plenty of individual variability. The political landscape includes lefties who own guns, right-wingers who drive Priuses and everything in between. There is also an unresolved chicken-and-egg problem: Do brains start out processing the world differently or do they become increasingly different as our politics evolve? Furthermore, it is still not entirely clear how useful it is to know that a Republican's brain lights up over X while a Democrat's responds to Y.

So what can the study of neural activity suggest about political behavior? The still emerging field of political neuroscience has begun to move beyond describing basic structural and functional brain differences between people of different ideological persuasions–gauging who has the biggest amygdala–to more nuanced investigations of how certain cognitive processes underlie our political thinking and decision-making. Partisanship does not just affect our vote; it influences our memory, reasoning and even our perception of truth. Knowing this will not magically bring us all together, but researchers hope that continuing to understand the way partisanship influences our brain might at least allow us to counter its worst effects: the divisiveness that can tear apart the shared values required to retain a sense of national unity.

Social scientists who observe behaviors in the political sphere can gain substantial insight into the hazards of errant partisanship. Political neuroscience, however, attempts to deepen these observations by supplying evidence that a belief or bias manifests as a measure of brain volume or activity–demonstrating that an attitude, conviction or misconception is, in fact, genuine. "Brain structure and function provide more objective measures than many types of survey responses," says political neuroscientist Hannah Nam of Stony Brook University. "Participants may be induced to be more honest when they think that scientists have a 'window' into their brains." That is not to say that political neuroscience can be used as a tool to "read minds," but it can pick up discrepancies between stated positions and underlying cognitive processes.

Brain scans are also unlikely to be used as a biomarker for specific political results because the relationships between the brain and politics is not one-to-one. Yet "neurobiological features could be used as a predictor of political outcomes—just not in a deterministic way," Nam says.

To study how we process political information in a 2017 paper, political psychologist Ingrid Haas of the University of Nebraska-Lincoln and her colleagues created hypothetical candidates from both major parties and assigned each candidate a set of policy statements on issues such as school prayer, Medicare and defense spending. Most statements were what you would expect: Republicans, for instance, usually favor increasing defense spending, and Democrats generally support expanding Medicare. But some statements were surprising, such as a conservative expressing a pro-choice position or a liberal arguing for invading Iran.

Haas put 58 people with diverse political views in a brain scanner. On each trial, participants were asked whether it was good or bad that a candidate held a position on a particular issue and not whether they personally agreed or disagreed with it. Framing the task that way allowed the researchers to look at neural processing as a function of whether the information was expected or unexpected—what they termed congruent or incongruent. They also considered participants' own party identification and whether there was a relationship between ideological differences and how the subjects did the task.

Liberals proved more attentive to incongruent information, especially for Democratic candidates. When they encountered such a position, it took them longer to make a decision about whether it was good or bad. They were likely to show activation for incongruent information in two brain regions: the insula and anterior cingulate cortex, which "are involved in helping people form and think about their attitudes," Haas says. How do out-of-the-ordinary positions affect later voting? Haas suspects that engaging more with such information might make voters more likely to punish candidates for it later. But she acknowledges that they may instead exercise a particular form of bias called "motivated reasoning" to downplay the incongruity.

Motivated reasoning, in which people work hard to justify their opinions or decisions, even in the face of conflicting evidence, has been a popular topic in political neuroscience because there is a lot of it going around. While partisanship plays a role, motivated reasoning goes deeper than that. Just as most of us like to think we are good-hearted human beings, people generally prefer to believe that the society they live in is desirable, fair and legitimate. "Even if society isn't perfect, and there are things to be criticized about it, there is a preference to think that you live in a good society," Nam says. When that preference is particularly strong, she adds, "that can lead to things like simply rationalizing or accepting long-standing inequalities or injustices." Psychologists call the cognitive process that lets us do so "system justification."

Nam and her colleagues set out to understand which brain areas govern the affective processes that underlie system justification. They found that the volume of gray matter in the amygdala is linked to the tendency to perceive the social system as legitimate and desirable. Their interpretation is that "this preference to system justify is related to these basic neurobiological predispositions to be alert to potential threats in your environment," Nam says.

After the original study, Nam's team followed a subset of the participants for three years and found that their brain structure predicted the likelihood of whether they participated in political protests during that time. "Larger amygdala volume is associated with a lower likelihood of participating in political protests," Nam says. "That makes sense in so far as political protest is a behavior that says, 'We've got to change the system.'"

Understanding the influence of partisanship on identity, even down to the level of neurons, "helps to explain why people place party loyalty over policy, and even over truth," argued psychologists Jay Van Bavel and Andrea Pereira, both then at New York University, in *Trends in Cognitive Sciences* in 2018. In short, we derive our identities from both our individual characteristics, such as being a parent, and our group memberships, such as being a New Yorker or an American. These affiliations serve multiple social goals: they feed our need to belong and desire for closure and predictability, and they endorse our moral values. And our brain represents them much as it does other forms of social identity.

Among other things, partisan identity clouds memory. In a 2013 study, liberals were more likely to misremember George W. Bush remaining on vacation in the aftermath of Hurricane Katrina, and conservatives were more likely to falsely recall seeing Barack Obama shaking hands with the president of Iran. Partisan identity also shapes our perceptions. When they were shown a video of a political protest in a 2012 study, liberals and conservatives were more or less likely to favor calling police depending on their interpretation of the protest's goal. If the objective was liberal (opposing the military barring openly gay people from service), the conservatives were more likely to want the cops. The opposite was true when participants thought it was a conservative protest (opposing an abortion clinic). The more strongly we identify with a party, the more likely we are to double down on our support for it. That tendency is exacerbated by rampant political misinformation and, too often, identity wins out over accuracy.

If we understand what is at work cognitively, we might be able to intervene and try to ease some of the negative effects of partisanship. The tension between accuracy and identity probably involves a brain region called the orbitofrontal cortex, which computes the value of goals and beliefs and is strongly connected to memory, executive function and attention. If identity helps determine the value of different beliefs, it can also distort them, Van Bavel says. Appreciating that political affiliation fulfills an evolutionary need to belong suggests we should create alternative means of belonging—depoliticizing the novel coronavirus by calling on us to come together as Americans, for instance. And incentivizing the need to be accurate could increase the importance accorded that goal: paying money for accurate responses or holding people accountable for incorrect ones have been shown to be effective.

It will be nearly impossible to lessen the partisan influences before the November 3 election because the volume of political information will only increase, reminding us of our political identities daily. But here is some good news: a large 2020 study at Harvard University found that participants consistently overestimated the level of out-group negativity toward their in-group. In other words, the other side may not dislike us quite so much as we think. Inaccurate information heightened the negative bias, and (more good news) correcting inaccurate information significantly reduced it.

"The biology and neuroscience of politics might be useful in terms of what is effective at getting through to people," Van Bavel says. "Maybe the way to interact with someone who disagrees with me politically is not to try to persuade them on the deep issue, because I might never get there. It's more to try to understand where they're coming from and shatter their stereotypes."

About the Author

Lydia Denworth is a Brooklyn, N.Y.–based science writer and a contributing editor for Scientific American. *She wrote about the neuroscience of stuttering in our August 2021 issue. She is co-author of* Parent Nation.

How Identity, Not Issues, Explains the Partisan Divide

By Cameron Brick, Sander van der Linden

U.S. politics increasingly looks like a savage battle between left and right. Consistent with closing ranks in a battle, Americans are expressing policy opinions that align more and more with their political groups. Of all conflicts between groups in America, partisanship is one of the most divisive, with 86% of Americans seeing strong conflicts between Republicans and Democrats. Yet, political differences are not always cause for alarm. Increased sorting could reflect identification with groups that better match our values. Perhaps Republicans and Democrats can't compromise because their policy preferences are irreconcilable. However, this doesn't explain why Americans personally dislike political opponents with such intense fervor.

U.S. liberals and conservatives not only disagree on policy issues: they are also increasingly unwilling to live near each other, be friends, or get married to members of the other group. This rejection based on group membership is called *affective polarization*, meaning that our feelings (affect) are different towards members of our own group compared to outsiders. Growing intolerance in the U.S. is a puzzle because disagreeing about policies need not cause rampant mistrust and legislative gridlock. For example, countries with proportional electoral representation like Germany create functional coalitions across different ideologies.

Now, surprising new research suggests that what divides us may not just be the issues. In two national surveys, political psychologist Lilliana Mason of the University of Maryland measured American's preferences on six issues such as abortion and gun control, how strongly they identified as liberals and conservatives, and how much they preferred social contact with members of their own ideological groups. Identifying as liberal or conservative only explained a small part of their issue positions. (This is consistent with findings that Americans overestimate the differences in policy preferences between Republicans and Democrats.) Next, Mason analyzed whether the substantial intolerance between liberals and conservatives was due to their political identities (how much they labelled themselves as "liberal" or "conservative") or to their policy opinions. For example, who would be more opposed to marrying a conservative: a moderate liberal who is pro-choice, or a strong liberal who is pro-life? Across all six issues, identifying as liberal or conservative was a stronger predictor of affective polarization than issue positions. Conservatives appear particularly likely to feel cold towards liberals, even conservatives who hold very liberal issue positions.

At the same time, the research has several important limitations. First, the study did not use an experimental design–it's based on surveys–so the results cannot speak to whether affective polarization causes partisan conflict. Moreover, the set of included policy issues was not comprehensive and may therefore underestimate the links between issue positions and identity or with outgroup dislike. Furthermore, expecting a strong link between ideology and issue positions ignores the fact that many individuals respond to political surveys by repeating what they've recently heard from media and political elites rather than reflecting on personal values. These observations can explain why Americans' issue positions often appear contradictory and unstable over time.

Nonetheless, we see that Americans are increasingly divided not just on the issues but also on their willingness to socialize across the political aisle. It is normal that society manifests new social cleavages as it heals old ones. However, when identities are fused with policies that have vast, long-term consequences (e.g., war, taxes, or the Paris Agreement), these divisions imperil our ability to select policies based on their expected outcomes. To paraphrase anthropologist John Tooby, forming coalitions around policy questions is disastrous because it pits our modest urge for truth-seeking against our voracious appetite to be good group members. If

Americans slide into seeing all policy debates as battles between Us vs. Them, we stop selecting policies based on their actual content. Ironically, this would lead to choosing policies that don't match our personal values, because the content and evidence would become less important than the source. In short, seeing politics as a battle may worsen things for everyone.

One solution might be to appeal to what psychologists call "superordinate identities." For example, Republicans and Democrats are both members of a larger unifying category: Americans. The common ingroup theory predicts that if members from opposing parties ("us vs. them") think about being part of the same group ("we"), partisans can develop more positive attitudes towards each other. As Martin Luther King is thought to have said: "We may have come on different ships, but we're all in the same boat now." Let's try to keep afloat.

About the Authors

Cameron Brick is a Research Associate in the Department of Psychology and the Cambridge Social Decision-Making Lab at the University of Cambridge.

Sander van der Linden is Assistant Professor of Social Psychology in the Department of Psychology at the University of Cambridge where he directs the Cambridge Social Decision-Making Lab. He is also a Fellow of Churchill College, Cambridge.

How the Sense of Taste Has Shaped Who We Are

By Gareth Cook

What is flavor? Beginning with this simple question, the Pulitzer prize-winning journalist John McQuaid weaves a fascinating story with a beginning some half a billion years ago. In his new book, *Tasty*, McQuaid argues that the sense of taste has played a central role in the evolution of humans. McQuaid's tale is about science, but also about culture, history and, one senses, our future. He answered questions from Mind Matters editor Gareth Cook.

Q: What made you decide to write a book about taste?

A: I have two kids, a boy and a girl born two years apart—now teens—and a few years ago, I became fascinated with how their tastes and preferences in food differed. My son liked extremes, especially super-hot chili peppers and whole lemons and limes. My daughter hated that stuff. She preferred bland comfort foods such as mashed potatoes, pasta, cheese and rice. White foods. Both kids were also picky eaters. They liked what they liked, and it didn't overlap (except for pizza). Speaking as a parent, this was maddening.

So I wondered where these differences came from. Were they genetic? The kids had mostly the same genes. Environment? They lived in the same place. And yet clearly both genes and environment were in play somehow. So I began to look into the question, and a whole world opened up.

And the basic answer to my original question is: kids are, biologically speaking, weird creatures. Pickiness seems to be programmed by evolution: it would have protected small children from eating strange, possibly poisonous items. Certain preferences, meanwhile, can develop arbitrarily and become very strong, then suddenly fade—every kid goes through phases as the brain matures and the neural networks that shape perception and behavior grow. Each person's sense of flavor is like a snowflake or a fingerprint, in this way, shaped partly by genes, but largely by experience. And always changing as more meals are eaten.

Q: What is known about the earliest origins of the sense of taste?

A: The sense of taste–or let's say taste and smell, the two big components of flavor–is impossibly ancient, dating back more than a billion years to the earliest cells, which needed to sense chemicals in the seawater around them–stuff to avoid, or stuff that was beneficial. So over time natural selection crafted receptor proteins. These are coiled molecules in cell walls that respond to specific kinds of chemical signatures (and also to light, vibration and other stimuli).

The really interesting thing is, as more complex life evolves–that is, multicellular life with mouths, brains, and internal organs–taste and smell play a central role. They are linchpins of survival, of winning the game of natural selection. They allow an animal to sense prey is nearby, and to derive some satisfaction from devouring it. The more acute they are, the better. And the more acute they become, the more brainpower is needed to process them. So the emergence of more sophisticated brains and behavior are, in evolutionary history, very often tied to sharpening senses of smell and taste. You can see this in anatomy: our systems for taste and smell are tied into the oldest, most "primitive" parts of the brain.

Q: You also draw connections between the sense of taste and the earliest humans. What did you find most interesting about this?

A: Flavor plays an underappreciated role the evolution of Homo sapiens, and in the invention of culture. How the human body evolved – the big brain, small gut, upright posture – is a hotly-debated topic. But a big driver is a series of dietary revolutions: from vegetarian to omnivore, from raw to cooked food. These go hand-in-hand with the use of tools, which were all about food: killing it, cutting it up, preparing it. And as tools improve, so does the food. Cutting and pounding meat or tubers tenderizes them. Cooking fires make everything more palatable and easier to digest. A positive feedback loop emerges between tastier food, better food, better tools, and changing bodies and brains.

Cooked game, for example, tastes vastly better than raw game. It's also a bigger challenge to obtain and to prepare than, say, jungle fruits. The hunt requires the ability to run, the right weapons, a complex strategy, cooperation. Meal prep requires the ability to render the meat, make a fire, roast and serve communally. As with earlier life forms, flavor is the crux of big evolutionary changes.

You also see one legacy of these changes in the shape of the human head. The retronasal passage running from the mouth up to the nasal cavity – where the aromatic component of flavor arises as food is chewed – shortened as human jaws shrank and faces flattened. The shorter distance supercharged flavors. So, although we have a weaker sense of smell than many other mammals, for us, smell plays a much more powerful role in flavor. Our big brains, meanwhile, allow flavor to tap into a range memories, thoughts, emotions and associations. This is what allows us to appreciate the fine flavors of braised meats, wines or cheeses.

Q: You mentioned your son's love of "extreme" tastes. What are some of the most extreme tastes you discovered in your reporting?

A: I took my son Matthew to visit Ed Currie, a South Carolina pepper grower who now holds the Guinness Book of World Records title for hottest chili in the world. It's called Smokin' Ed's Carolina Reaper. There is a lively and competitive subculture in the United States and around the world devoted to breeding ever-hotter chili peppers. Just in the past five years, the record has changed hands several times and the spiciest peppers are now twice as hot as they used to be. It's quite a phenomenon. There's no good biological explanation for why anybody likes chili heat–a form of irritation or pain. It's more a matter of psychology, perhaps a form of thrill-seeking or so-called "benign masochism." How far can it go? Are there physical limits to how much heat we're willing to endure?

We tried very tiny slivers of the Carolina Reaper, and a few other super-hot varieties. The sensation builds for about 15 to 20 seconds, then becomes unbearable on the tongue and elsewhere in the mouth. You feel it through your whole body–the molecule behind the sensation, capsaicin, binds to heat receptors and taps into the body's temperature regulation system. Fortunately, capsaicin has another feature: after a few minutes, it starts shutting down the nerves it has inflamed, and the pain dulls. Which means you can try some more! Our host, meanwhile, was eating entire peppers without breaking a sweat – you can develop a tolerance for the heat.

Another time, my family and I went to Iceland, where we tried hákarl, which is the fermented meat of the Greenland shark. It's a national dish, yet considered one of the most disgusting foods in the world. Vikings originally buried shark meat for months in the sand; today it's placed in wooden crates with weights on top, to squeeze out toxic chemicals that exist naturally in the flesh. After a few months of this and some curing, it smells like a combination of rotting fish and ammonia. We put small chunks in our mouths, and the ammonia pretty much overwhelmed everything. My daughter spit it out.

Many cultures have this type of food: beloved at home and reviled everywhere else. This shows how powerful conditioning is: the human brain can learn to like almost anything under the right circumstances. This is a legacy of our ancestors' experience as hunter-gatherers colonizing habitats everywhere on earth. Sometimes, you had to learn to like some new food just to stay alive.

Q: How can our sense of taste be used against us?

A: Flavor is an eminently corruptible sense. It is a very old part of the brain's motivational architecture. This is what the pleasure in a scoop of ice cream, or a sip of single malt scotch, really is: a motivational nudge, a behavioral reward. You can't separate pleasure from flavor, and yet they're not exactly the same thing – pleasure in food waxes and wanes depending on the circumstances. A lot of today's foods—particularly junk food and the menus of chain restaurants—are about bombarding the brain's pleasure circuits with sensations. Some of this is the unholy trinity of sugar, salt, and fat. Some of it is strong or evocative spices engineered to stand out, because humans also crave variety and contrast in food.

Keep overloading any system, and eventually it gets out of whack. It's similar to addiction. Persistently overindulge, the same amount of some treat doesn't taste quite as good, so you eat more to make up for it. This corruptible aspect of flavor affects diet, eating habits, self-image, your whole life.

Q: What is the future of taste?

A: I wish I knew! So much is happening, so fast, compared to the last 100 years, or the last 10,000. Two thoughts. One is that we're at a dangerous juncture. Food companies now employ geneticists and neuroscientists. Yet the technology for making new foods and outré flavors far outstrips our understanding of brain or body. So we're running a massive experiment.

But it's also a very exciting time. Take fermentation. For hundreds of thousands of years, alcoholic beverages, cheeses, pickles, sauerkraut, tofu, kimchi and other fermented foods and drinks were made using traditional recipes. But no one understood the biology of how the yeasts, fungi and bacteria involved in fermentation made flavor. The actual molecules that create many fine sensations are almost always very numerous and obscure, the result of microbial metabolisms churning away. But now scientists are developing a better understanding of how those metabolisms work, and the ability to manipulate them. This will open up vast new domains of deliciousness. In many respects, we're just getting started on the taste adventure.

About the Author

Gareth Cook is a Pulitzer Prize–winning journalist who edits Scientific American's *Mind Matters online news column.*

Dissecting the Bloodthirsty Bliss of Death Metal

By David Noonan

Brutality now becomes my appetite
Violence is now a way of life
The sledge my tool to torture
As it pounds down on your forehead

Shakespeare it's not. Those lyrics, from "Hammer Smashed Face" by the band Cannibal Corpse, are typical of death metal—a subgenre of heavy metal music that features images of extreme violence and the sonic equivalent of, well, a sledgehammer to the forehead.

The appeal of this marginal musical form, which clearly seems bent on assaulting the senses and violating even the lowest standards of taste, is mystifying to non-fans—which is one reason music psychologist William Forde Thompson was drawn to it. Thompson and his colleagues have published three papers about death metal and its fans this year, and several more are in the works.

"It's the paradox of enjoying a negative emotion that I was interested in," says Thompson, a professor at Macquarie University in Sydney, Australia. "Why are people interested in music that seems to induce a negative emotion, when in everyday life we tend to *avoid* situations that will induce a negative emotion?" A number of studies have explored the emotional appeal of sad music, Thompson notes. But relatively little research has examined the emotional effects of listening to music that is downright violent.

Thompson's work has produced some intriguing insights. The biggest surprise? "The ubiquitous stereotype of death metal fans—fans of music that contains violent themes and explicitly violent lyrics—[is] that they are angry people with violent tendencies," Thompson says. "What we are finding is that they are not angry people. They're not enjoying anger when they listen to the music, but they are in fact experiencing a range of *positive* emotions."

Those positive emotions, as reported by death metal fans in an online survey that Thompson and his team conducted, include feelings of empowerment, joy, peace and transcendence. So far, almost all of the anger and tension Thompson has documented in his death metal studies has been expressed by non-fans after listening to samples of the music.

In a paper titled "Who enjoys listening to violent music and why?" published earlier this year in *Psychology of Popular Media Culture*, Thompson and colleagues sought to identify specific personality traits that distinguished death metal fans from non-fans. In the study, which involved 48 self-described death metal fans and 97 non-fans (all in their 20s), he deployed an arsenal of established psychological tools and measures. These included the Big Five Inventory (BFI) of personality–which assesses openness to experience, conscientiousness, agreeableness and neuroticism–as well as the Interpersonal Reactivity Index (IRI), a 28-item measure of empathy.

Notably, on measures of conscientiousness and agreeableness, the scores of death metal fans were subtly but reliably lower than those of non-fans. One possible explanation for this finding, the authors write, "is that long-term, persistent exposure to violent media may lead to subtle changes in one's personality, desensitizing fans to violence and reinforcing negative social attitudes." But Thompson emphasizes that we just don't know. It is also possible that people with these personality traits are more likely to gravitate to death metal.

Results from the IRI showed the fan group and non-fan group with similar scores on the four dimensions of empathy that the index measures. When listening to death metal, however, study participants with lower empathy scores were more likely to experience higher levels of power and joy than those with greater empathic concern. That was true as well, Thompson found, for people whose personality assessment showed them to be more open to experience and less neurotic.

In the study, each participant listened to four out of eight 60-second samples of popular death metal songs (selected by the researchers from multiple online lists) and answered questions about the feelings the music evoked. The songs included "Slowly We Rot," by Obituary and "Waiting for the Screams," by Autopsy, as well as "Hammer Smashed Face."

In one set of responses, the subjects rated (on a scale of 1 to 7) the emotional effects of the music, using pre-selected terms such as "fear" and "wonder." In a second step, they described in their own words how death metal made them feel. "With its repetitive, fast-paced tempo, down-tuned instruments and blast beats, it is virtually impossible not to be excited!" one fan wrote. "It sounds like messed-up teenagers making throaty, irritating noises about how bad their lives are," wrote a non-fan. "It's annoying."

The fact that the study relies on self-reporting by the subjects is a red flag for Craig Anderson, a psychology professor at Iowa State University who has spent his career researching the links between media violence and aggression, and who was not involved in Thompson's study. Self-reporting "may or may not reflect reality," Anderson says. "People may be lying to you, or, more likely, people don't have direct access to many of the kinds of effects that media have on them. They can construct an idea or hypothesis, and self-reports are essentially that kind of data. People may report that 'Oh yeah, this makes me feel this way,' without recognizing whether that's really true."

The paper acknowledges the limitations of self-reporting. But the researchers add that "the convergence of evidence" from the personality assessments and other measures, along with the fans' enthusiastic embrace of death metal, "suggest that the dramatic differences in emotional and aesthetic responses between fans and non-fans are genuine.

Chris Pervelis, a founding member and guitarist of the band Internal Bleeding (whose songs include *Gutted Human Sacrifice* and *The Pageantry of Savagery*), is confident that the positive emotions he experiences when he plays and listens to Death Metal are the real thing. "When I'm locked into it, it's like there's electricity flowing through me," says the 50-year-old, who runs his own graphic design business. "I feel really alive, like hyper-alive. And the people I know in Death Metal are smart, creative and generally good-hearted souls."

In an essay published in August in *Physics of Life Reviews*, Thompson and his co-author Kirk Olsen considered the possible role of brain chemistry in the response to violence and aggression in music. The high amplitude, fast tempo and other discordant traits of death metal, they write, may elicit the release of neurochemicals such as epinephrine–which "may underpin feelings of positive energy and power reported by fans, and tension, fear and anger reported by non-fans."

As for the central riddle of death metal–how explicitly violent music might trigger positive emotions in some people–Thompson cites a 2017 paper on the enjoyment of negative emotions in art reception, published in *Behavioral and Brain Sciences*. The paper, from the Max Planck Institute for Empirical Aesthetics, suggests a mental process that combines "psychological distancing" and "psychological embracing." In other words, a lack of real-world consequences–it's just a song!–may provide the *distance* necessary for fans to appreciate the music as an art form and *embrace* it.

A large body of research, by Anderson and others, has established a clear link between aggression and multiple types of media violence including video games, film, television and music with violent images and themes. "But no one is saying that a normal, well-adjusted person–who has almost no other risk factors for violent behavior–is going to become a violent criminal offender simply because of their media habits," says Anderson, whose research includes a 2003 study of the effect of songs with violent lyrics. "That never happens with just one risk factor, and we know of dozens of common risk factors. Media violence happens to be one."

One finding from Thompson's research–that many death metal fans say they listen to the music as a catharsis, a way to release negative emotions and focus on something that they enjoy–is also familiar to Pervelis. "I call it the garbage can," he says of the music he's been involved with for decades, "because it's where I can dump all my bad, emotional baggage. I put it into writing riffs and letting it all out on stage, and it keeps me level and completely sane."

In his ongoing study of violent and aggressive music, which includes a June paper in the journal *Music Perception* about the intelligibility of death metal lyrics (forget about it, non-fans), Thompson has found that the limited appeal of the form may be one its key features for fans–one at least as old as rock itself. He cites a 2006 paper by the late Karen Bettez Halnon, who found that fans of heavy metal (as has certainly been the case with many other genres and sub-genres over the decades) view the music as an alternative to the "impersonal, conformist, superficial and numbing realities of commercialism."

In that vein, one possible function of the gruesome lyrics that are the hallmark of death metal, says Thompson, may be to "sharpen the boundary" between fans and everybody else. Pervelis, who compares the violent imagery to the "over-the-top, schlock horror films of the 70s," says feeling like an outsider and an insider at the same time is at the core of the death metal experience. "This music is so extreme and so on the fringe of the mainstream that people who listen to it and people who play in death metal bands belong to an elite club. It's like we've got a little secret, and I think that's what binds it all. It's a badge of honor."

About the Author

David Noonan is a freelance writer specializing in science and medicine.

Section 4: The Factors that Shape Your Personality

More Than Meets the Eye: The Evolution of Personality Testing

By Heather Myers

If you've taken a personality test before, you know it can be a tedious and frustrating process. The prospect of answering countless and repetitive questions leaves people disengaged–yet these tests continue to be taken by millions every year. Recruiters, HR professionals and psychologists use them to assess things like how someone might fit into a company's culture, people's leadership styles, areas of potential growth, or simply how groups work together. Indeed, the science behind these applications is well established with models of personality such as the Big Five having 50 years of research behind them.

However, as new HR technologies emerge, traditional tests seem increasingly out of touch. Why? Because the user experience is often incredibly poor. Many tests still involve pencil and paper, and almost always endless word-crunching. The bigger problem is that they don't tap into what we humans are best at: visual processing.

Visual tests are not completely new. Image-based tests like the Rorschach inkblot test, which unearths unconscious (and often consciously embarrassing) aspects of the human psyche, have long been used by psychologists to explore personality. New generations of image-based tests do not rely on ambiguous stimuli, but instead use images in different ways. Leutner and colleagues developed a measure of creativity that uses text-based questions, but replaces a text rating scale with a series of two to eight images. The user then responds to the images. Traitify, where I serve as chief psychology officer, takes another approach and has created a user-friendly and mobile assessment using the Big Five model. These use a series of images accompanied by brief captions. Users then simply click "Me" or "Not Me" at the bottom of the image.

The use of images in personality assessments makes them more fun, seamless and engaging, but also has other added benefits. First, using image-based assessments can reduce test taker fatigue because processing pictures requires less attention than processing text and is much, much faster. In fact, Potter and colleagues found that the brain can process the complex information within an image in only 13 milliseconds. This is a staggering 60,000 times faster than processing text alone! The reduction in test fatigue can lead to more accurate responses and better completion rates.

Second, images not only tap into conscious processes extremely quickly but they also access the unconscious, and elicit faster and stronger preferences. Responses to images are more likely to be definitive. Third, image-based assessments are easier to digest for those who have difficulty reading or understanding text. This should make them more accessible to those with learning difficulties, less education or language barriers. Finally, a stronger reliance on images as opposed to text may be the better approach when trying to understand personality across cultures. Carefully selected images don't require the kind of fine-tuning across languages and cultures that text requires, and are thus less prone to cultural misunderstandings.

Given the potential benefits of using images in assessment, it isn't surprising that test designers have begun to use pictures and even videos. As an example, researchers are even beginning to explore the use of assessments that mimic video games to predict the success of orthopedic surgical residents. Although more work is needed to establish the full validity of the new generation of visual assessments, initial research looks promising. One thing is certain: we must find creative and interesting ways to measure personality and keep up with people's increasing expectations of emerging technology.

Visual tests like these are becoming more common and critical now more than ever before, thanks to the evolution of technology and increase in new behaviors and usage of devices. A report on media consumption from University of California, San Diego estimates that we consume information for an average of 12 hours a day, bombarding our brains with 34 gigabytes of data per day, which requires more internal, human processing than ever before. Mobile phones are a major contributor to the rise in information consumption and it's only going to increase with 5 billion global mobile users by 2019. In addition, people in emerging economies like China, India and Africa are using mobile phones as their only means to access the internet.

Rather than stick to traditional methods, it's imperative that we start to embrace the benefits of mobile technology–allowing people to take and use image-based personality tests, quickly and simply, wherever they are in the world. Technology will continue to advance steadily as will the expectations of job applicants. Using advancements like image-based tests to capitalize on seemingly obvious facts (humans are best at visual processing!) will become the norm. Companies ignoring these trends will quickly get left behind.

The views expressed are those of the author(s) and are not necessarily those of Scientific American.

About the Author

Heather Myers holds a PhD in personality psychology and a master's degree in statistics from Stanford University. With more than 15 years of experience in the field, she serves as Traitify's chief psychology officer where she develops personality assessments and runs and analyzes validation studies.

A Long-Running Study Finds People's Characters Don't Remain Fixed

By Melinda Wenner Moyer

Many studies suggest that our personalities remain fairly stable, even over the course of decades. Yet a small but long-running study finds that traits related to dependability differ substantially between adolescence and late life. The findings raise new questions and highlight the challenges inherent in trying to track a person's defining characteristics over many years.

In the new research, published in December 2016 in *Psychology and Aging*, researchers in the U.K. reached out to a group of 635 77-year-olds from Scotland who had taken part in a study when they were 14. Back then, their teachers had rated them on six personality characteristics related to dependability: self-confidence, perseverance, mood stability, conscientiousness, originality and desire to excel. Some 60 years later a total of 174 participants from the original cohort rated themselves on the same six traits and had a close friend or relative rate them as well.

Lead author Ian Deary, a psychologist at the University of Edinburgh, expected, based on earlier findings, that dependability scores might remain stable over time. In fact, he and his colleagues found no relation between ratings for dependability-related traits over the 63-year span studied. (Deary emphasizes that his findings apply only to these six traits–not overall personality.)

One of the study's strengths is that it covers such a long period, but this characteristic also makes the research challenging. Nate Hudson, a social psychologist at Michigan State University who was not involved in the study, points out that the lack of personality stability could be an artifact of having different people rate the participants. Ideally, the same person would rate a subject's personality at both time points when assessments were made.

In decades-spanning studies, many subjects go missing, die or choose not to participate in follow-up assessments. Deary and his colleagues enrolled only 174 of the original participants, a number that makes it tough to find subtle, but real, correlations in sets of data. "It is difficult to know from their study alone whether there is truly zero stability in personality from age 14 to 77," Hudson says. Deary's work moves the field forward—but more research is needed to get a full picture of how personality evolves throughout a lifetime.

About the Author

Melinda Wenner Moyer, a contributing editor at Scientific American, *is author of* How to Raise Kids Who Aren't Assholes: Science-Based Strategies for Better Parenting—From Tots to Teens *(G. P. Putnam & Sons, 2021).*

How Accurate Are Personality Tests?

By Angus Chen

If you're looking for insight into the true you, there's a buffet of personality questionnaires available. Some are silly–like the internet quiz that tells everyone who takes it that they are procrastinators at the core. Other questionnaires, developed and sold as tools to help people hire the right candidate or find love, take themselves more seriously.

The trouble is, if you ask the experts, most of these might not be worth the money. "You should be skeptical," says Simine Vazire, a personality researcher at the University of California, Davis. "Until we test them scientifically we can't tell the difference between that and pseudoscience like astrology."

One famous example of a popular but dubious commercial personality test is the Myers–Briggs Type Indicator. This questionnaire divides people into 16 different "types" and, often, the assessment will suggest certain career or romantic pairings. It costs $15 to $40 for an individual, but psychologists say the questionnaire is one of the worst personality tests in existence for a wide range of reasons. It is unreliable because a person's type may change from day to day. It gives false information ("bogus stuff," one researcher puts it). The questions are confusing and poorly worded. Vazire sums it up as "shockingly bad."

Personality questionnaires began evolving about a century ago, says Jim Butcher, an emeritus psychologist at the University of Minnesota. "They started asking questions about an individual's thinking and behavior during World War I," he says. "These were to study personality problems and mental health problems." And importantly, he adds, the U.S. military wanted the questionnaires to help weed out soldiers who weren't fit to fly military aircraft.

According to Butcher, during the first half of the 20th century many academics started creating different personality scales. "Not just on mental health diagnoses, but what personality is like," he says. The problem with practically all of the assessments at the time was they were a built on the creators' subjective feelings about personality, he notes. "Then people started to raise questions about do they really measure what they think they're measuring? How reliable are those conclusions, and are they valid?"

Butcher describes what followed as a mass culling of personality systems and questionnaires by the scientific method. There is one personality model that did survive the 20th century, though. It is popular among academics today, and is what Vazire uses in her research. It's called the Big 5 Personality Traits (aka 5-Factor Model), and it was developed over three decades beginning in 1961 at Brooks Air Force Base. From then to the 1990s, several psychologists including Lewis Goldberg, Warren Norman, Paul Costa and Robert McCrae helped develop the model into its modern form.

Vazire says in developing the Big 5 Personality model, psychologists tried to avoid pitfalls that plagued early personality researchers–like selecting criteria based primarily on intuition. Instead, the Big 5 model took a holistic tack by compiling every word that could be considered a personality trait and creating simple, straightforward questions about them. For example, on a scale of 1 to 5, are you outgoing, sociable? Have a forgiving nature? Based on how people answered initial surveys, researchers used statistical methods to group traits that seemed to cluster together (like "talkative" and "sociable") into five basic categories: extraversion, conscientiousness, agreeableness, neuroticism and openness to experience. The other model, the HEXACO model of personality structure created in 2000 by psychologists Kibeom Lee at the University of Calgary and Michael Ashton at Brock University in Ontario, is similar but adds an extra category: honesty–humility.

The key to the Big 5 model is its simplicity. It doesn't sort anybody into a "type," just informs them where they fall on a continuum of personality traits. There are no tricks and no surprises to be revealed, Vazire says. "In a way, it's disappointing. It just means that personality tests can only tell you what you tell it." You won't learn anything that you didn't already know about yourself, she adds, and its accuracy comes entirely from how honest and self-reflective you were with your answers.

At best, Vazire says you could use it as a comparative tool that can tell you how you rank on extroversion compared with others who have taken the same test. There have been studies that show certain Big 5 factor scores correlate with certain outcomes—conscientiousness correlates with longer life, for instance, and extroversion correlates with higher sales for sales reps. "But that doesn't mean someone with high extroversion will be a better salesperson," Vazire says. Correlations are just that; they could be incidental. But commercial personality assessments seem to depend heavily on such correlations. For example, one assessment from The Predictive Index, a company that measures behavioral characteristics and matches personality profiles to jobs, views such correlations in their own studies as a measure of success. "[We showed] in one client, a retail jeweler, that increases in dominance or aggression was responsible for $125,000 in revenue," says Thad Peterson, one of the company's executives. The idea behind The Index, Peterson says, is to use those measures to help "marry people to [job] positions."

Such personality assessments—particularly those targeted toward hiring recruiters and managers—aim to uncover a kind of "hidden truth about the person," says Randy Stein, a psychologist at California Polytechnic State University, Pomona. "They assume that there is an essence of you and an essence of the job, and you should be matching up those two things in hiring," he says. "But I don't think there is a hidden truth—and even if there is, a personality test doesn't do it."

Like the Big 5 model, any personality or behavior assessment can't know things you haven't explicitly answered in the questionnaire, Stein says. Sometimes commercial personality tests ask odd questions—like, Do you identify with snakes? or How do you react to a certain color?—and try to draw inferences from your answers. Those kinds of conclusions venture into the pseudoscientific, Stein says.

There are other reasons why Stein thinks some personality assessments may be pseudoscientific. "What those tests will tell people is true or false is determined by what people are willing to pay for," he says. "Their process as a company is to tell people whatever will sell the product." By contrast, the Big 5 and HEXACO models were shaped by an empirical process and independent peer review that showed people's scores tended to be consistent, and predictions made using the models are reproducible. Without that, Stein says personality tests should be treated with extreme suspicion.

Some companies like The Predictive Index say their product meets such standards. The company invested in an audit, paying over $20,000 dollars to Norwegian classification firm DNV GL to review their product and certify that it complies with a standard set by the European Federation of Psychologists' Associations. Two Index representatives, Greg Barnett and Austin Fossey, also say predictions based on their methods are accurate.

Perhaps. U.C. Davis's Vazire says it is fairly easy to reach some level of validity. "If I just asked you to make a questionnaire on extroversion, you would probably do a pretty good job," she says. It is because we are all judges of character, and we often do well at intuiting whom to date or hire and who we are, Vazire says. If the process seems confusing or if questions veer off into the abstract, that's a red flag. Personality, she says, is just not that mysterious.

Most of Us Combine Personality Traits from Different Genders

By Spencer Greenberg, Holly Muir

How different are men and women *really*? About 30 years ago, if dating guides are any indication, some people assumed vast differences in personality, with *Men Are from Mars, Women Are from Venus* relationship advice. Today, in contrast, certain communities are pushing back against the idea of binary gender, which presents men and women as separate categories. (A quick reminder: gender–described in terms such as "man," "woman" and "nonbinary person"–has strong cultural and social components. But sex–sometimes described with adjectives such as "male," "female" and "intersex"–refers to a combination of biological features.)

Scientists are also taking harder looks at gender, sex and personality. For one, researchers are debating how big the personality differences between cisgender men and women truly are. (These are people who describe themselves as either a man or a woman and say that this gender identity aligns with their sex assigned at birth.) The answer depends on how psychologists measure an individual's characteristics.

For example, a study involving more than 300,000 people in the U.S. who self-identified as either male or female looked both at broad personality traits, such as extraversion and agreeableness, and at more specific aspects of these traits, such as a warm communication style or a tendency to act altruistically. In this sample, researchers found moderate differences between male and female participants in the broad traits but, in most cases, larger differences at the more specific level. Overall, for instance, both male and female people in the study were similarly extraverted (a broad trait). When the scientists looked at specific aspects of extraversion, however, they found that male participants, on average, sought out exciting situations more often than female ones did. And female participants demonstrated higher activity levels than male ones.

To test the most comprehensive set of personality traits to date, our project, ClearerThinking.org, ran a series of 15 studies and conducted analyses on more than 15,000 people. Our analyses are limited to cisgender men and women: 98 percent of the participants in our research identified themselves this way, so we did not have enough data to shed light on the personality traits of nonbinary and transgender people. From the data, we discovered 18 specific self-reported traits that varied between these men and women. Next, we built an algorithm designed to predict a person's gender based on their self-reported scores on those traits, which was accurate 78 percent of the time. That accuracy is high but far from perfect, revealing the challenge of predicting an individual's gender from their combination of traits. Finally, we adapted our study questionnaire–in which people rated how much they agree with statements such as "I laugh aloud" and "I frequently worry"–into an online interactive assessment.

To create the questions for our studies, we cast a very wide net, looking at large personality projects, reviewing the academic literature and crowdsourcing ideas. We ended up testing more than 600 personality questions for gender differences before identifying the 18 traits with the greatest variation between the self-identified men and women in our sample. These traits included not only the broad characteristics that are widely used in psychological research (such as extraversion and agreeableness) but also more specific patterns of thought and behavior, such as how frequently an individual takes risks or their degree of focus on aesthetics. We also double-checked our conclusions by running a final study to replicate the major findings. Ultimately we found no large differences in personality between cisgender men and women on any traits. But we did find small and moderate differences in the 18 personality traits.

The most sizable of these differences was the degree to which cisgender people thought about sex, assessed by asking people to rate how much they agreed with the statement "I often have sexual thoughts when I meet an attractive-looking person" and disagreed with the statement "I do not frequently think about sex." (This "sex-focused" characteristic, while not linked to major personality traits commonly studied in psychology, nonetheless fits the conception of a personality trait as a pattern in thought, emotion or behavior. It also relates to a concept called sexual preoccupation.) We found that gender could explain about 18 percent of the variation in the extent to which people are sex-focused. Men had a higher average score on this trait than women. There were still plenty of women who had a higher score than most men, however. In other words, individual men and women were highly varied, even though at the group level, men tended to differ from women.

On every trait, there was a substantial overlap between men and women. Yet at the tail ends–where people either strongly agreed or disagreed with the questions we asked them–larger differences emerged. For example, very low compassion was rare in both men and women, but the few people who identified as very uncompassionate were much more likely to be men. This result is consistent with the finding that antisocial personality disorder, which often involves a lack of remorse or empathy, is more common among men than women.

So is there a "man's personality" and a "woman's personality"? Fascinatingly, almost everyone in our study was a mix of "more often seen in men" and "more often seen in women" traits. For any given trait, an individual woman was closer to the overall average for women than the overall average for men just 61 percent of the time. And a man was closer to the average for men than the average for women only 57 percent of the time. Only about 1 percent of men and 1 percent of women had almost entirely "more often seen in men" or "more often seen in women" personality traits.

To test how accurately gender can be predicted from personality, we developed a simple machine-learning algorithm (a computer program that looked for patterns in data regarding which personality traits are associated with being a cis man or a cis woman). We trained our algorithm using results from past study participants, then presented the algorithm with the personality traits of new participants to see how well it could predict their gender. Using just the most predictive trait–being sex-focused–the algorithm could predict a person's gender correctly 69 percent of the time. This result may be impressive to some. But the prediction is far from perfect because some women are much more sex-focused than the average man.

The algorithm's accuracy rose to 78 percent when we allowed it to incorporate all the personality differences at once. That's a big improvement–but for the other 22 percent of people, the algorithm was predicting incorrectly. When we released our quiz to the public, accuracy slipped a bit further to 74 percent. That's still much better than the average human, though: We gave another group of study participants sets of personality traits that, we explained, belonged to particular individuals. Then we asked the participants to predict the gender of those other people using the personality traits. They were correct only 58 percent of the time, hardly better than a coin flip. The quiz is called the Gender Continuum Test, and you can try it yourself on our website to see whether the algorithm predicts your gender.

We believe our results shed new light on the size of gender differences in personality. There are, however, some important caveats. First, all our study participants were from the U.S., and given that factors such as culture influence personality and gender, we would be hesitant to extend our conclusions to other communities. Second, our study cannot provide insight into the *causes* of personality differences–for instance, how much these differences can be explained by environment and culture as opposed to biology. Third, as we noted earlier, we do not have enough data to comment on transgender, intersex or nonbinary individuals. We hope that future research explores these and other dimensions of the personality, sex and gender debate.

Right now our study is a reminder that, on average, cisgender men and women do have some small to moderate differences in how they report their personality, but almost everyone is a mix of traits seen more often in men *and* seen more often in women. If you try to guess someone's personality from their gender, you'll very often be wrong.

About the Authors

Spencer Greenberg is a mathematician and founder of ClearerThinking.org.

Holly Muir is a researcher at ClearerThinking.org who specializes in developing interventions for critical thinking.

Personality Type, as Well as Politics, Predicts Who Shares Fake News

By Asher Lawson, Hemant Kakkar

Behavioral and political scientists have pointed fingers at political conservatives, as opposed to liberals, when it comes to spreading fake news stories. But not all conservatives do it, and sweeping generalizations threaten to condemn everyone who subscribes to conservative values. This approach risks even more dangerous polarization.

Political leanings are far from the only determinants of behavior. Personality is a crucial influence, so our research on misinformation sharing has focused on that. One widely used psychological system for identifying personality traits organizes them into five categories: openness to experience, conscientiousness, extroversion, agreeableness and neuroticism. (It is called, unsurprisingly, the five-factor theory.) We looked specifically at conscientiousness, which captures differences in people's orderliness, impulse control, conventionality and reliability.

In a series of eight studies with a total of 4,642 participants, we examined whether low-conscientiousness conservatives (LCCs) disseminate more misinformation than other conservatives or low-conscientiousness liberals. First we determined people's political ideology and conscientiousness through assessments that asked participants about their values and behaviors. We then showed the same people a series of real and fake news stories relating to COVID and asked them to rate how accurate the stories were. We also asked whether they would consider sharing each story.

Both liberals and conservatives sometimes saw false stories as accurate. This error was likely driven in part by their *wanting* certain stories to be true because they aligned with their beliefs.

But actually sharing false news was markedly higher among LCCs compared with everyone else in the study, although some people of all persuasions did it. There was no difference between liberals and conservatives with high levels of conscientiousness. Low-conscientiousness liberals did not share more misinformation than their high-conscientiousness liberal counterparts.

What explains the exceptional tendency of LCCs to share fake news? To explore this question, we gathered information about participants' politics and personalities and administered questionnaires to assess their need for chaos—the desire to disrupt and destroy the existing political and social institutions—as well as their support of conservative issues, support for Donald Trump, trust in mainstream media and time spent on social media. LCCs, we learned, expressed a general desire for chaos, and this need may explain their proclivity to spread misinformation. Other factors, including support for Trump, were not as strongly related.

Unfortunately, our work on this personality trait also suggests that accuracy labels on news stories will not solve the problem of misinformation. We ran a study where we explicitly stated whether each news story in question was false, using a "disputed" tag commonly seen on social media, or true, using a "supported" tag. We found that the supported tag increased the rate at which real stories were shared among both liberals and conservatives. LCCs, however, continued to share misinformation at a greater rate despite the clear warnings that the stories were false.

We ran another study that involved explicitly telling participants that an article they wanted to share was inaccurate. People then had the chance to change their choice. Not only did LCCs still share fake news at a higher rate than others in the study, but they also were comparatively insensitive to direct warnings that the stories they wanted to share were false.

The poor effectiveness of warnings among LCCs is worrying because our research suggests these people are primary drivers of fake-news proliferation. Social media networks therefore need to find a different solution than just tagging stories with warning labels. Interventions based on the assumption that truth matters to readers may be inadequate. Another option might involve social media companies monitoring fake news that has the potential to hurt others, such as misinformation related to vaccines and elections, and actively removing such content from their platforms.

Whatever the case, until these companies find an approach that works, this problem will persist. In the interim, our society will pay the cost of spreading misinformation. The long, conspiratorial road that rioters followed to the January 2021 Capitol insurrection shows that this spread can have serious and damaging consequences.

About the Authors

Asher Lawson is a graduate student in Duke University's Management and Organizations program.

Hemant Kakkar is an assistant professor of management at Duke University's Fuqua School of Business. His research draws on social psychology and evolutionary theories of status and influence to examine judgments and behaviors of individuals and groups within social hierarchies.

A Change to the Sound of the Voice Can Change Your Very Self-Identity

By Guillaume Jacquemont

The voice is the human musical instrument. It consists of a vibrating element, resonating chambers and energy that produces the vibrations. The energy comes from the breath originating in the lungs. Vibrations occur in the two vocal cords at the lower part of the voice box, or larynx, that are arranged in a "V" shape, perpendicular to the trachea. Finally, the resonating chambers consist of multiple structures located above the vocal cords: the upper part of the larynx, the pharynx, the nasal cavity, the mouth.

Our voice is the only musical instrument that is both a string and a wind instrument–as the breath causes the vocal cords to vibrate. It is almost an orchestra unto itself. All this gives each of us a particular, unique vocal imprint; there are seven billion humans, seven billion different voices. *Scientific American*'s French-language sister publication *Cerveau & Psycho* talked about the wonders of the voice to the Paris-based Jean Abitbol, an ear, nose and throat physician, phoniatrician and craniofacial surgeon.

[*An edited transcript of the interview follows.*]

Q: How important is the voice to a person's self-identity?

A: It is indeed an essential component. We see this very clearly when we operate on patients to change their voice; their self-identity is strongly disrupted. For example, I met a lawyer who had a very deep, masculine voice because of an edema on her vocal cords caused by her smoking. (She smoked two packs of cigarettes a day.) She had a great charm and authority in her profession, where she interacted with criminals on a daily basis. ("My world is the prisons; I defend all the thugs," she told me.) But she wanted to change her voice, which her fiancé didn't like, and asked me to operate on her. I advised her to change her fiancé instead! She burst out laughing and had the operation done by a colleague.

When I saw her again, she had a very high-pitched voice and told me something terrible: "I am schizophrenic about my voice." She no longer recognized herself when she spoke, and was seized by the impression that "it wasn't her," that it was someone else speaking. The consequences were terrible: her fiancé had left her, she could no longer work, she lost all her court cases, she had no authority, she no longer dared to open her mouth in prison.... Not because her voice had become higher pitched, but because there was a sort of rupture of harmony with who she was, a conflict with herself, a feeling of loss of identity that destabilized her. She started smoking again, recovered her voice in two or three years and gradually regained influence in her professional life.

Q: I imagine that a change in your voice is also disturbing to people around you.

A: That's well put. Imagine that from one day to the next, your spouse or your children no longer sound the same. This is what happened to one of my patients, a 36-year-old woman. She had suffered from vocal cord paralysis since the age of nine or 10 following a viral infection of the vagus nerve, which controls the vocal cords. This gave her a voice like a whisper, with no power. She had to use a bell to call her husband or children!

I injected her with a substance that allows the vocal cords to become flexible again, and she recovered in two weeks. But she no longer recognized herself: "Doctor, I have a woman's voice!" She had never known this voice before, since her paralysis dated back to before puberty. The experience was still very positive for her. She no longer felt like a strange beast. But her family felt unsettled. After the operation, her husband asked me a question with some irritation in his voice: "What have you done to her? She's not my wife anymore." The same goes for her children:

"She's not Mom anymore!" Two months later, having gotten used to the change, they came to apologize and tell me that they thought it was great; but their first reaction had been to feel usurped, as if something had been stolen from them.

All of this illustrates the extreme caution that must be exercised before making changes to the voice apparatus. It's emotional surgery. When you have appendicitis, you operate on it, but if you detect a growth on the vocal cords, if it is not cancerous and does not bother the patient, why touch it? I knew the ENT specialist who treated Louis Armstrong. Armstrong had vocal cords with two enormous masses that probably gave him that hoarse voice with inimitable evocative power. Imagine if they had been removed.

Q: You mentioned "emotional surgery." Could you tell us more about the relationship between voice and emotion?

A: Our emotions are like the conductor of our voice. If you smile, if you're not feeling well, if you're anxious, all of this can be heard, because of very concrete consequences to your vocal apparatus. The lubrication of the vocal cords is very good when you feel good, but it is much less so when you're anxious, stressed or have stage fright. The blood supply also deteriorates in the latter case, notably because of a contraction of the blood vessels. The vocal cords then whiten and lose their flexibility, which translates into a dryness in the voice. In addition, frequent and intense stress causes gastric reflux in the vocal cords, which dry out due to the acidity and become covered with bumps (keratosis). As a result, the voice breaks and becomes hoarse. Emotional expressions also modify the configuration of the vocal resonance chambers, notably by mobilizing the mouth and cheeks.

Because of these things, we can't accurately recreate a voice synthetically. Even if projects to do this at the National Conservatory of Arts and Crafts (Conservatoire National des Arts et Métiers) achieve remarkable technical performances, the emotional side is missing. Conversely, the great opera singers, such as Luciano Pavarotti or Maria Callas, had an exceptional talent for conveying emotions.

Q: What other facets of our identity are expressed in the voice?

A: Our social identity, for example. A lawyer or a doctor doesn't speak like a politician. This is expressed through language, of course, but also through components of the voice, such as the rhythm of speech. Perhaps the man who illustrated this most vividly was Charlie Chaplin in his film *The Great Dictator*: when the character who parodies Hitler addresses the crowd from his balcony, even though he doesn't actually speak a word of German, his speech immediately evokes a political harangue and an authoritarian leader. The voice also betrays our gender, since it clearly differs between men and women. It is no coincidence that many transgender people want to change their voice.

Q: Why do men and women have such different voices?

A: Mainly because of the hormonal influx at puberty, testosterone causing a lengthening and thickening of the vocal cords (which are about 24 millimeters long and four to five millimeters wide in men, and 18 millimeters long and three to four millimeters thick in women), as well as an enlargement of the resonance box of the larynx. This is why *castrati*, who were for a long time made to sing in operas, had to be operated on before puberty. This did not give them a woman's voice, but a child's voice, even higher than that of a woman. If their voice was so out of the ordinary and had such power, it is because the growth hormones and the thyroid hormone, which are produced by glands other than the testicles and which are under the influence of the Y chromosome, gave them the morphological size and the respiratory strength of a man.

Apart from this particular case, a man's voice generally has predominantly low pitches and a woman's high pitches. The low and high notes always coexist in both sexes and enhance each other, like a diamond and its case. Because the beauty of a voice is its depth.

Q: Are there many people who are not comfortable with their voice and want to change it?

A: No, not really. It's rare that someone comes to me with such a request. And in 95 percent of cases, I send them to a psychologist because it's a sign that they have a problem with themselves. For example, a 40-year-old woman with a thin, broken voice recently asked me to operate on her. But when I examined her, I discovered a magnificent vocal apparatus. She then revealed to me that her problem dated back to the day after she lost her mother, who she said had an exceptional voice. There was nothing I could do. It was up to a psychologist to intervene.

In most cases, the desire to change one's voice in a profound way betrays an underlying psychological problem. Without wanting to change it completely, many people want their voice to be more persuasive, to have a certain power. The importance of the voice in communication has long been known, but the desire to control its power has increased tenfold with COVID-19 and the advent of telecommuting, with virtual meetings. A voice coach can help. In the end, what these people want to change is not their voice itself, but the way they use it.

This article originally appeared in Cerveau & Psycho *and was reproduced with permission.*

About the Author

Guillaume Jacquemont is an editor at Cerveau & Psycho *and author of* La Science des Reves (The Science of Dreams), *Flammarion, 2020.*

GLOSSARY

algorithm A process that is followed in order to solve a problem or make a calculation, especially by a computer.

amygdala Almond-shaped masses of nuclei located in the temporal lobes of the human brain that play an important role in emotion, memory, and decision making.

caveat A warning about the conditions or limitations of something in order to prevent misinterpretation.

coercive Using threats or force to persuade people to do things against their will.

gender dysphoria Distress or unease that occurs when the gender assigned to a person at birth does not match one's gender identity.

essentialism The view that a set of attributes or characteristics are necessary and unchangeable parts of one's identity.

implicit bias Automatic and unintentional stereotypical judgment or behaviors that occur without one's conscious knowledge.

incongruent Incompatible, not in keeping with other aspects.

influx Flowing in or increasing in number.

microaggression A commonplace and subtle interaction or behavior that suggests hostility or other negative feelings toward someone of a marginalized group. It can be an intentional or unintentional act.

predisposition Susceptible or more likely to do something or be a certain way.

subconscious Related to a part of the mind that one is not aware of but that impacts behavior.

underpinning The foundational theories, ideas, or beliefs that justify or support something.

FURTHER INFORMATION

American Psychological Association. "Personality: Where Does It Come From and How Does It Work?" *ScienceDaily*, 14 February 2018, www.sciencedaily.com/releases/2018/02/180214150202.htm.

Cherry, Kendra. "Are Personality Traits Caused by Genes or Environment?" *Verywell Mind*, 27 April, 2020, https://www.verywellmind.com/are-personality-traits-caused-by-genes-or-environment-4120707.

Harmon, Amy. "BIPOC or POC? Equity or Equality? The Debate Over Language on the Left," *New York Times*, 1 November 2021, https://www.nytimes.com/2021/11/01/us/terminology-language-politics.html.

Kaufman, Scott Barry. "Can Personality Be Changed?" the *Atlantic*, 26 July, 2016, https://www.theatlantic.com/health/archive/2016/07/can-personality-be-changed/492956/.

Klein, Ellora. "The Psychology of Taste: The Intertwining of Music and Identity," *Science Survey*, 14 June 2021, https://thesciencesurvey.com/arts-entertainment/2021/06/14/the-psychology-of-taste-the-intertwining-of-music-and-identity/.

Lambert, Jonathan. "No 'Gay Gene': Study Homes in on Genetic Basis of Human Sexuality," *Nature*, 29 August 2019, https://www.nature.com/articles/d41586-019-02585-6.

Vanderbilt, Tom. "The Psychology of Genre," *New York Times*, 28 May 2016, https://www.nytimes.com/2016/05/29/opinion/sunday/the-psychology-of-genre.html.

Warren, Sasha. "People May Pick Friends Who Smell Like Them," *Scientific American*, 24 June 2022, https://www.scientificamerican.com/article/people-may-pick-friends-who-smell-like-them/.

CITATIONS

1.1 What Drives Subconscious Racial Prejudice? by Jeneen Interlandi (May 11, 2015); 1.2 How to Unlearn Racism by Abigail Libers (October 1, 2020); 1.3 Stereotypes Harm Black Lives and Livelihoods, but Research Suggests Ways to Improve Things by Katy Milkman, Kassie Brabaw (July 8, 2020); 1.4 The Science of Microaggressions: It's Complicated by Scott Lilienfeld (June 23, 2017); 1.5 How to Think about 'Implicit Bias' by Keith Payne, Laura Niemi, John M. Doris (March 27, 2018); 1.6 The Flexibility of Racial Bias by Mina Cikara, Jay Van Bavel (June 2, 2015); 1.7 The Problem with Implicit Bias Training by Tiffany L. Green, Nao Hagiwara (August 28, 2020); 1.8 To Fight Bias, Consider Highlighting Your Race or Gender by Erika Kirgios, Aneesh Rai, Edward Chang, Katy Milkman (March 28, 2022); 2.1 Doctors Must Dig into Gender Difference to Improve Women's Health Care by Marcia L. Stefanick (September 1, 2017); 2.2 Is There a "Female" Brain? by Lydia Denworth (September 1, 2017); 2.3 Promiscuous Men, Chaste Women and Other Gender Myths by Cordelia Fine, Mark A. Elgar (September 1, 2017); 2.4 When Sex and Gender Collide by Kristina R. Olson (September 1, 2017); 2.5 The Disturbing History of Research into Transgender Identity by Jack Turban (October 23, 2020); 2.6 What the Science on Gender-Affirming Care for Transgender Kids Really Shows by Heather Boerner (May 12, 2022); 2.7 The Search for a 'Cause' of Transness Is Misguided by Nat Mulkey (March 23, 2021); 3.1 In Teen Music Choices, Anxiety Rules by Abigail Baird (March 16, 2010); 3.2 Conservative and Liberal Brains Might Have Some Real Differences by Lydia Denworth (October 26, 2020); 3.3 How Identity, Not Issues, Explains the Partisan Divide by Cameron Brick, Sander van der Linden (June 19, 2018); 3.4 How the Sense of Taste Has Shaped Who We Are by Gareth Cook (January 13, 2015); 3.5 Dissecting the Bloodthirsty Bliss of Death Metal by David Noonan (October 30, 2018); 4.1 More Than Meets the Eye: The Evolution of Personality Testing by Heather Myers (January 24, 2018); 4.2 A Long-Running Study Finds People's Characters Don't Remain Fixed by Melinda Wenner Moyer (May 1, 2017); 4.3 How Accurate Are Personality Tests? by Angus Chen (October 10, 2018); 4.4 Most of Us Combine Personality Traits from Different Genders by Spencer Greenberg, Holly Muir (January 31, 2022); 4.5 Personality Type, as well as Politics, Predicts Who Shares Fake News by Asher Lawson, Hemant Kakkar (November 12, 2021); 4.6 A Change to the Sound of the Voice Can Change Your Very Self-Identity by Guillaume Jacquemont (November 1, 2021)

Each author biography was accurate at the time the article was originally published.

Content originally published on or after July 1, 2018, was reproduced with permission. Copyright 2023 Scientific American, a Division of Springer Nature America, Inc. All rights reserved.

Content originally published from January 1, 2010, to June 30, 2018, was reproduced with permission. Copyright 2023 Scientific American, a Division of Nature America, Inc. All rights reserved.

Content originally published on or before December 31, 2009, was reproduced with permission. Copyright 2023 Scientific American, Inc. All rights reserved.

INDEX